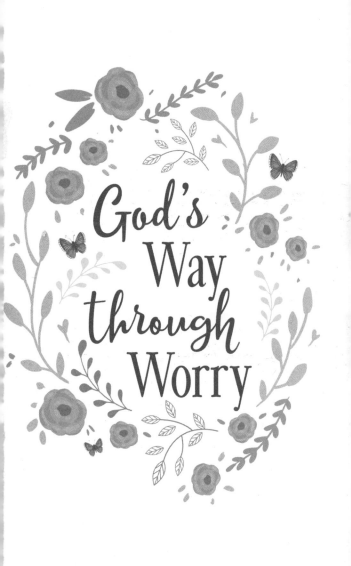

God's
Way
through
Worry

JANICE THOMPSON

God's Way through Worry

90 Empowering
Devotions for Women

BARBOUR
PUBLISHING

ISBN 978-1-64352-801-4

Published by Barbour Publishing, Inc., 1810 Barbour Drive, Uhrichsville, Ohio 44683, www.barbourbooks.com

Our mission is to inspire the world with the life-changing message of the Bible.

 Member of the
Evangelical Christian
Publishers Association

Printed in China.

Nothing is impossible with God.

Your heavenly Father is a Waymaker—the ultimate Navigator who makes a way even when there seems to be no way through the situations in your life. He loves you deeply and wants the very best for you, which means He will stop at nothing to see you through.

If you're like most women, you still fret when seemingly impossible situations come along. You look at them and say, "There's just no way. I'll never get through this. This mountain is too high. That valley is too deep. The situation I'm facing is completely impossible to navigate, let alone overcome." You often forget that your Waymaker is already on the job, putting things in place.

Lift your head, precious woman of God! This collection of devotions was written for you—for those seasons when worries seem bigger than God, when impossibilities seem overwhelming. God is your Waymaker. He *will* make a way. No matter how long you've been fretting, He'll step in and take care of the details if you let Him.

Through these devotions, you will see that your Creator thrives on the impossible. What you cannot do, He can! When you throw up your hands and say, "I can't!" He steps in and says, "Oh, but I can. . .and I will!"

God will make a way. . .and He's ready for you to anticipate that even now.

A Way through the Sea

Moses answered the people, "Do not be afraid.
Stand firm and you will see the deliverance the
Lord will bring you today. The Egyptians you see
today you will never see again. The Lord will
fight for you; you need only to be still."
Exodus 14:13–14 niv

Moses stared at the vast sea before him, his
heart in his throat. No doubt worry lines creased
his forehead as he grasped the rod in his hand.
Six hundred of Pharaoh's best chariots, filled
with Egyptian officers, were barreling up behind him. If God didn't move—and soon—the
Israelites would be overtaken and killed. Their
hopes of a Promised Land would be over.

Moses lifted his rod and held it up, an act of
pure faith and determination. As he stretched
his hand out over the sea, the Lord drove the
waters back with a strong east wind, and the
Israelites passed over to the other side on dry
land. The Egyptians, thinking they would be
just as safe, followed suit. But God released the

waters, and the Egyptian army met its demise that day.

God made a way for the Israelites through a seemingly impossible situation. He crafted a plan. And when the Lord crafts a plan, it exceeds human expectation and comprehension.

No doubt you've faced impossible situations in your life. They've loomed before you like a vast sea of troubles. You've contemplated the many ways you might navigate to the other side, but the situation seemed impossible. Then God, with a single breath, blows back the waters and makes a way for you to cross over. He's truly a miracle worker!

No matter how troubled you are right now, He will make a way. Get ready to step into His plan. You can trust Him because He loves you.

Father, I know You've already made a way.
I can trust Your plan. Please navigate this
situation for me, I pray. Amen.

From Worry to Faith

*Now faith is confidence in what we hope for
and assurance about what we do not see.*
HEBREWS 11:1 NIV

Jenna tossed and turned in the bed. She couldn't stop thinking about the stack of bills sitting on the bedside table. The electricity was scheduled to be shut off in a few days. She could pay the bill right now, but doing so would mean she'd have to juggle her rent payment. . .again.

She continued to toss and turn, knotted up with anxiety. Finally, she sat up in bed and turned on the lamp. Jenna took the bills into her hands and—instead of fretting over them— began to pray. She prayed for God's provision but also for His wisdom to know how to better handle her finances.

When she finished praying, Jenna set the bills aside, turned off the lamp, and dozed off. She awoke with a new determination to do things God's way. Several phone calls later, she came up with a plan to navigate her way

through this month's bills, which would buy her a bit of time to tackle the larger problems.

With the help of a credit counselor, Jenna finally managed to get her situation under control. She moved out from under a mountain of debt and was finally free to release the anxiety.

Maybe you've walked a mile in Jenna's shoes. You twist the sheets at night, riddled with worry over the bills. Don't give up! God is a Waymaker, a miracle worker. As long as you come to Him ready to make things right, He will make a way even if you created the mess. He wants you to walk in complete freedom, so trust Him in this.

Lord, I give my finances to You! I'm sorry for the mess I've made, Lord. I can't undo what I've done, but I repent and ask for Your help. Please make a way, Father. Amen.

A Nail in the Can

Commit your work to the LORD,
and your plans will be established.
PROVERBS 16:3 ESV

A young missionary was attempting to explain to the local natives how Jesus Christ went to the cross and offered Himself as a sacrifice for their sins. When he reached the part of the story about the nails piercing Jesus' hands and feet, he ran into a dilemma. . .these natives didn't understand the word *nail*. They had never seen one. The missionary tried his best to explain through the interpreter but closed the message feeling frustrated.

He quietly slipped away to the side of a cool creek to rest for a while and think. The over-heated gentleman reached down into the cold water and, as was his habit, pulled up several cans of orange juice that he had tied to a string and immersed several hours earlier to cool. He chose a particular can, opened it, and began to drink. As he sipped the cool juice, he thought

about his dilemma and wondered what he might say to make the people understand. He took one last swallow then heard a light *clink* coming from inside the can. Surprised, he turned it over, and out dropped a small nail!

Can you imagine? Somewhere in Florida, a worker had accidentally dropped a nail into a can of juice. That particular case of juice was shipped to California, where the missionary's sister had purchased it at a local grocery store. From there, she sent the case to the remote area of the world where the missionary was stationed. That particular morning, the missionary had chosen several cans of juice, submerging them all in the cool creek. When he pulled them out of the water, he chose the very can that held the nail!

God made a way for this missionary through a seemingly impossible situation. Do you think He will do less for you?

Thank You, Lord, for putting a nail in my (proverbial) can! I can trust You with all my worries, Lord. Amen.

Seeds Planted in Advance

A man was there by the name of Zacchaeus;
he was a chief tax collector and was wealthy. He
wanted to see who Jesus was, but because he was
short he could not see over the crowd. So he ran
ahead and climbed a sycamore-fig tree to see
him, since Jesus was coming that way.

LUKE 19:2–4 NIV

"I can't help it if I'm short," Zacchaeus sighed as the crowd formed in front of him. The one they called Jesus would be coming down the road soon, and if Zacchaeus stood any chance of seeing him firsthand, it wouldn't be back here, pressed behind the masses.

He craned his neck and looked around until he noticed a sycamore tree on the side of the road. With all the strength he could muster, he climbed up, up, up into its branches. Funny, no one on the ground below seemed to notice, not that he cared. He caught a glimpse as the Master drew near. And, boy, was he shocked when Jesus looked straight up at him and said, "Zacchaeus,

come down from that tree! I'm going to your house today!" Whoa. Talk about unexpected.

God made a way for Zacchaeus. Long before Zacchaeus encountered Jesus that day, God planted a seed that would grow into a tree sturdy enough to hold a grown man. Talk about planning everything in advance.

God will make a way for you too. You don't know what you'll need tomorrow. . .or next year . . .or the year after that. But the Lord knows, and He's already planting the seeds.

God, You knew what Zacchaeus needed, and You know what I need. I'm so grateful for Your provision. Thank You for planting seeds even before the need arises. Amen.

Love and Faithfulness

Let not steadfast love and faithfulness
forsake you; bind them around your neck;
write them on the tablet of your heart.
PROVERBS 3:3 ESV

A broken marriage. Friendships betrayed. Kids who had turned on her and gone their separate ways. Alice wondered if she would ever be able to trust anyone again. Did all relationships end in unfaithfulness, or was she just unlucky enough to latch on to people who broke her heart? It seemed to happen again and again—in her love life, with her friends, and even at work. Did she have the worst luck, or what? And if it was her fault, how could she fix it? Was there some magic relationship cure?

Maybe you can relate to Alice's plight. You've had your heart broken a time or two. You've been devastated by someone you trusted, even loved. You worry that your next friendship will end the way the last one did. Or you're scared to give your heart to another man because you're

convinced he'll just break it. You can't help but wonder if there are any faithful people left in the world. Are you the only one capable of keeping your word?

God wants you to know that He will never cheat on you. He'll never betray you. He'll never let you down in any way. And when people fail you, He'll be right there to mend your broken heart and to help you make a way through the stress and anguish of it all. He's your Waymaker and will make a way through these worries and concerns you're facing over broken relationships. Trust Him. He's got this.

Lord, I'm so glad I can trust in You.
You have my best interests at heart even when
others don't. I'm so grateful, Lord. Amen.

Where You Go, I'll Go

But Ruth said, "Do not urge me to leave you or to return from following you. For where you go I will go, and where you lodge I will lodge. Your people shall be my people, and your God my God."
RUTH 1:16 ESV

Picture yourself in Ruth's shoes. A young widow, leaving your family to travel with your widowed mother-in-law to her homeland. You know no one. You have nothing. Your only real link to the woman (her son, your husband) is now deceased. And yet you feel compelled to go with her for whatever reason.

So you commit yourself. Where you go, I'll go. Where you stay, I'll stay. Your people will be my people, your God, my God. Whew. That's a pretty big commitment!

You arrive in Israel, her homeland not yours, and find yourself in need of help. So, you head to the field of her relative, Boaz, and ask if you can glean the leftovers. He agrees. You spend your days following behind the

harvesters, picking what you can so that you will not starve.

Then your mother-in-law asks you to do the impossible: Go to Boaz. Ask him to cover you, to take you on as his wife. You're terrified. Your knees are knocking. You don't really know this man. He owes you nothing. But off you go to the one person who can save you.

And save you, he does! Miraculously, he commits to taking you as his own. You become his wife and eventually the mother of his child. And all because you overcame your worries, your concerns, and stepped out in faith.

You're much like Ruth. You step out in faith, committing yourself to God. He gives you a task and then covers you with His great love. Step out in faith. Your Waymaker has already ordered your steps.

Thank You, Father, for covering me!
I'm so grateful for Your provision. Amen.

A Sleepless Night

*Do not be anxious about anything, but in
everything by prayer and supplication with
thanksgiving let your requests be made known
to God. And the peace of God, which surpasses
all understanding, will guard your hearts
and your minds in Christ Jesus.*
PHILIPPIANS 4:6–7 ESV

Marian tossed and turned in bed, her thoughts
twisted as tight as a coil. The disconnect notice
from the electric company had her in a panic.
Two days. . .and the lights would be shut off.
Two days. How would she ever come up with the
money in that amount of time? It seemed impossible, given her current financial situation.

Imagine her surprise to find an unexpected
check in the mail the very next day. God had
miraculously met her need. And to think, that
check had already been written and mailed
before she spent a sleepless night worrying. . .
for nothing!

Maybe you've struggled with fears in the

night like Marian. You've wondered if your power would be shut off or if you'd turn on the faucet to discover no water. It's hard not to fret when you're facing inevitable deadlines. Having faith is even harder in the dark.

Here's some good news: God knows about those deadlines, and He cares very much about the things that matter to you. He knows you're worried; but remember. . .He always has an answer long before your worries begin. The key during these deadline-induced panics is to trust. Praise Him even before you see the provision. The next time you're faced with a sleepless night, count your blessings and then doze off.

Lord, I can trust You. You've already made
a way even when I don't see it. You're my
provider, Father, and I'm so grateful for the
sweet peace You give me day and night. Amen.

A Way through Grief

Be kind to one another, tenderhearted, forgiving one another, as God in Christ forgave you.
EPHESIANS 4:32 ESV

If anyone understood what it was like to forge a way where there seemed to be no way, it was Elisabeth Elliot, wife of missionary Jim Elliot. She lived through the unthinkable. Her husband's life was taken by members of the Auca tribe (a native tribe from Ecuador) while he was trying to share the Gospel. Elisabeth was wrecked by the news. How could she navigate the road after her husband's death? Should she stay on the mission field or head home to the States? What did God have in store for her as a grieving widow? There were so many decisions to make.

Over a period of years, God began to nudge open the door of her heart and make a way through the pain and unforgiveness. She not only forgave the men who killed her husband but actually ended up leading them into a saving

relationship with the Lord. God not only walked her through the worry, the pain, the grief; He also showed her how to forgive and minister to those who'd taken her husband's life and broken her own heart. Before long, the very men who had killed Jim were counted among her friends. Can you imagine?

Her Waymaker made a way through a situation that seemed absolutely impossible. If He could do that for Elisabeth, if He could turn her story around and bring new life, new hopes, new possibilities, imagine what He will do for you!

Lord, what a story! Elisabeth was an amazing woman of faith. Show me how to trust You like she did. I want to keep my eyes on You, my Waymaker! Amen.

Stepping up to the Plate

"Honor your father and your mother,
that your days may be long in the land
that the LORD your God is giving you."
EXODUS 20:12 ESV

Abby didn't feel cut out to be a caregiver, but life thrust her into that role, whether she wanted it or not. When her elderly mother was diagnosed with Alzheimer's disease, someone had to step up. Abby was the obvious choice, being the only one of her siblings who was a widowed empty nester. So, off to Mama's she went, ready to offer the best care possible. When she first started, things weren't too bad. Her mother's symptoms were manageable. At times Abby even questioned whether or not her mom was really sick. Then something would happen to remind her, and she would struggle with her emotions.

As her mother's condition progressed, Abby quickly found herself overwhelmed. There were so many decisions to be made, and she wasn't

sure she was making the right ones. How could she manage someone else's life and still keep her own health in check? It seemed impossible. At some point, she had to get over her fears and face reality: she had no other choice.

Maybe you've walked a mile in Abby's shoes. You had no choice but to step up to the plate and care for a loved one in need—a friend with cancer, a parent with memory issues, a child with chronic health problems. You became the advocate. You pressed your worries and fears aside and, with God's help, did what needed to be done. What a blessing you are!

Lord, I'm so grateful for my parents and other elderly friends and loved ones You've placed in my life. May I always treat them with the love and respect they deserve. Amen.

Fiery Trials

Shadrach, Meshach, and Abednego answered
and said to the king, "O Nebuchadnezzar,
we have no need to answer you in this matter.
If this be so, our God whom we serve is able to
deliver us from the burning fiery furnace,
and he will deliver us out of your hand, O king.
But if not, be it known to you, O king, that
we will not serve your gods or worship the
golden image that you have set up."
DANIEL 3:16–18 ESV

Have you ever felt like you were walking through
the fire? Maybe things in your life were so painful, so consuming, that you feared you would be
scorched beyond recognition. No one understood what that felt like more than Shadrach,
Meshach, and Abednego, the three Hebrew
youth who were thrown into a fiery furnace
because they refused to bow down to the king.
In their case, they marched bravely into the
furnace, not knowing if they would ever return.
If they died, they had given their lives to the

24

cause of faithfulness to God. They were willing to do that.

But they didn't die. God made a way through their situation. In fact, when they came out of the flames, they didn't even have the smell of smoke in their hair.

The same is possible with and for you. You'll go through fiery trials. No doubt about it. You'll likely fret and worry and wonder how you can possibly survive. But God, in His miraculous way, will bring you through it. He can make a way even through the flames! In fact, He'll bring you through without the lingering smell of smoke. In other words, He'll deliver you so completely that the pain of the past won't be a constant reminder. What an amazing heavenly Father, to see you through!

Lord, I trust You to bring me through the fiery trials. If You could rescue those three Hebrew boys, surely You can rescue me! Amen.

Broken Friendships

*A man of many companions may come
to ruin, but there is a friend who
sticks closer than a brother.*

PROVERBS 18:24 ESV

Jenny paced her bedroom, her heart in her throat. Her best friend, Mary, was angry at her. Really angry. She hadn't meant to upset Mary, but something Jenny said hit Mary the wrong way, and now she had shut down completely. Was the friendship over, or was this something they could get past? Jenny couldn't help but worry.

Maybe you've worried about broken friendships too. Perhaps you had a major falling-out with someone you used to be close to. She's moved on. You've tried to move on, but something is nagging at you. Guilt, perhaps? Grief?

You've spent countless hours playing and replaying the tapes in your head: what you said, what you should have said, how your friend responded, how you reacted to her response.

Ugh. If only you could go back and do it again.

Broken friendships are the worst! A severed relationship, especially between two people who've always been close, is hard to bear. But God sees. He knows. And He's the best at mending the unmendable, fixing the unfixable. He specializes in putting broken things back together even when it seems impossible.

Lean in. Listen to His voice. See what He's telling you today. Are you supposed to write a note of apology? Reach out in some other way? Bake cookies, perhaps? That wall will eventually fall if you stay tuned in to God's still, small voice. Your Waymaker is standing by, ready to bring reconciliation.

Lord, You are the mender of all, even broken friendships. I trust You, my Waymaker, to bring total healing in this relationship. Amen.

He Still Opens Doors

*And Hannah prayed and said, "My heart
exults in the LORD; my horn is exalted in
the LORD. My mouth derides my enemies,
because I rejoice in your salvation."*
1 SAMUEL 2:1 ESV

Overcome with emotion, Hannah knelt at
the altar. How could she bear the pain of
being childless any longer? Her enemy, Peninnah, continued bragging about her ability
to bear children. She rubbed it in at every possible opportunity. And Hannah did her best
to take it all in stride, but the desire to have a
child caused her grief to escalate to the breaking point. And she had to acknowledge her
jealousy too. She was jealous that Peninnah
was able to have children when she could not.

Maybe you've struggled with anxiety over
your inability to have a child as well. Perhaps
you've poured out so many tears, prayed so many
prayers, given up so many dreams that you are
convinced it will never happen.

Give those worries to God even if you've done so a hundred times before. He doesn't want you to give up on your dream. He has His own way of making dreams come true, so trust in Him. Don't let your worries get the best of you. He'll make a way even if there seems to be no way. Don't box Him in. Don't tell Him how to accomplish it. Chances are pretty good the plan He has for you will far exceed your expectations. Remember, He's the great door opener, the amazing miracle worker. And He always keeps His promises.

Trust, woman of God. His time. His way. His plan. Amen?

Lord, I trust You even in this. That's the hardest thing to say, but I do believe Your plan far exceeds my own. Make a way, I pray, Father. Amen.

A Way through the Pain

"For I know the plans I have for you, declares
the L<small>ORD</small>, plans for welfare and not for evil,
to give you a future and a hope."
J<small>EREMIAH</small> 29:11 <small>ESV</small>

Meredith eased herself to a sitting position. She swung her legs over the side of the bed and attempted to stand. The usual pain in her hips and legs made the task nearly impossible. Why did she suffer so much? Would it ever end? Mornings were usually the worst. It was so hard to get going. Why didn't God just zap the pain, take it away? Wouldn't that be a more gracious response than expecting her to plow through it?

Maybe you've fretted over chronic pain too. Perhaps it's joint pain. Maybe it's muscular. Perhaps you are struggling with chronic headaches or migraines. Perhaps you're struggling with an ongoing illness or disease. You wonder if things will always be like this. Does God really care?

It's hard to understand why some people,

especially good people, suffer so much. And it's easy to get down in the dumps about it—to grow anxious or worry that the pain will never end. The enemy would love nothing more than to see you give up, to allow your worries and fears to consume you. But the Lord is gracious. He loves you so much and won't give you more than you (with His help) can bear.

Don't give up your faith. God will make a way through the pain. He'll help you overcome those worries too. Trust Him through the pain to the other side.

Lord, even in my pain I choose to trust You. You're reminding me that You love and care about me and that You'll make a way through all of it. I'm counting on it, Father! Amen.

Trusting in the Jungle

*"I have said these things to you, that in
me you may have peace. In the world
you will have tribulation. But take
heart; I have overcome the world."*
JOHN 16:33 ESV

David Livingstone was an amazing Scottish
physician who was used greatly by God during
his years in the African jungle. A pioneer missionary, explorer, and antislavery crusader, he
accomplished remarkable things for God and
for the people he met along the way.

Things weren't always easy for David, as you
might imagine. He left all he knew and loved to
go to an unfamiliar and dangerous place far, far
away. (Can you picture it?) And the struggles
in Africa were almost insurmountable at times.
He could have left. . .permanently. But he was
drawn to the continent and the people. Even
during the hardest of times, God never left his
side. He saw David through struggles beyond
anything we could ever imagine.

You're not David Livingstone. Likely, you haven't been called by God to travel to distant shores or risk your life sharing the Gospel message or exploring unknown regions. But you've faced struggles, worries, and pains that feel as real (and sometimes dangerous) to you as those David faced in the jungle. In many ways, you've trekked through jungles of your own—heartaches, pains, losses, and financial woes.

Trust in the same God whom David trusted. When you're not sure of the road ahead, allow Him to guide you. And remember, if He could make a way through the jungles of Africa for an explorer, God can surely take care of you.

Lord, I'll trust You even in the jungles. When I'm nervous and upset, when I can't see my way, I'll remember that You are the best possible guide. I put my faith in You, my Waymaker. Amen.

You Are Wanted

Casting all your anxieties on him,
because he cares for you.
1 PETER 5:7 ESV

As an infant, Kathleen was adopted into an amazing home. Her adoptive parents never hid the fact that she wasn't their biological child, and she was always treated like their own. She was loved, cared for, and always adored just like the other children in the family.

Still, in spite of their best efforts, Kathleen struggled with abandonment issues. She couldn't pinpoint why she struggled, but troubling thoughts nagged at her: "Why did my birth mom give me up?" "Is there something wrong with me?" "Why don't I seem to fit in?" "Will I ever be loved. . .really truly loved. . .and wanted?" "Will these feelings of abandonment go on forever?"

It took some counseling and plenty of encouragement from her adoptive parents, but Kathleen eventually came to grips with her

worries and concerns. She learned to take them at their word when they said they loved—and wanted—her.

Maybe you've struggled with feelings of abandonment too. They're like a giant chasm in your life, and you've wondered if you'll ever get to the other side. Today God wants you to know that He's your Waymaker. He already has a plan to rid you of those nagging thoughts that you're not enough or that you aren't wanted. With His help, you'll make it through the emotions, worries, and concerns you're facing now. You *are* wanted. . .by Him and by plenty of others as well. Your life has value. You matter.

Thank You, my Waymaker, for reminding me that I'm wanted. Help me lay down my worries and concerns and remain convinced that You adore me, Lord. Amen.

God, Your Provider

"As surely as the LORD your God lives,"
she replied, "I don't have any bread—only
a handful of flour in a jar and a little olive
oil in a jug. I am gathering a few sticks to
take home and make a meal for myself
and my son, that we may eat it—and die."
1 KINGS 17:12 NIV

She had nothing. Only a handful of flour in a
jar and a little olive oil in a jug. And here stood
a prophet in front of her, asking for food. How
could she give him what she did not have? It
would take an act of faith to prepare food for
him with her remaining ingredients. When
faced with this monumental decision, she had
someone else to consider too. Her son. Would
she really feed a stranger before considering her
own child? The idea of leaving her boy hungry
left a knot in her stomach.

The widow woman, in an extreme act of
faith, chose to fix a final meal for Elijah. When
she stepped out in faith to do as he had asked, a

miraculous thing happened—her jar of oil did not deplete itself, and the flour level remained the same no matter how much she used. She and her son had food for days! Wow!

When was the last time you had to trust God for an honest-to-goodness miracle of provision? If He asked you to give from your point of need, would you? It's an act of faith, for sure, but if you pass the test, you can't imagine how He will bless you. He is your Waymaker and longs to see your needs met.

Lord, I trust You to provide when my cupboard is full or when it's nearly bare. I won't worry about where the next meal will come from. You've got this. I know You are trustworthy. Amen.

Cluck-Cluck-Clucking

Anxiety in a man's heart weighs him down,
but a good word makes him glad.
PROVERBS 12:25 ESV

A person who frets is visibly and often consistently anxious. Some would say, "She has a nervous personality," or "She always seems to be on edge."

In many ways, a fretter is like a hen that won't stop clucking. That fretful bird marches around the yard, digging, scratching, clucking. . .fretting. She's not making any progress. Her tirade solves nothing. But somehow all the noise makes her feel better. On and on she goes, her complaints, fears, and worries spilling off her tongue like water rolling over the falls, crashing onto the rocks below. Never mind the fact that she's exhausting those around her, wearing them down with her never-ending clucking. They're certainly not feeling better. And ultimately, neither is she.

The fretting might relieve her for a moment, but it's not a long-lasting solution.

Don't be a clucker. Don't pace and scratch. The Bible says that such behavior weighs you down. Instead, turn your gaze upward. Instead of fretting, speak words of faith over your situation. Remember, God isn't activated by fretting. That clucking doesn't motivate Him one bit. He's activated by praise and words of faith! So, begin to speak boldly. It will change your perspective and will save those around you a lot of grief. No one likes a clucking hen, after all.

Lord, I'm sorry for the years I've wasted clucking and fretting. I didn't mean to lose so much time agonizing over things I couldn't fix. You're the fixer, Lord, and I'll begin to praise You even now. Thanks for caring, Father. Amen.

Times of Desperation

Hezekiah turned his face to the wall and prayed to the LORD, "Remember, LORD, how I have walked before you faithfully and with wholehearted devotion and have done what is good in your eyes." And Hezekiah wept bitterly.
2 KINGS 20:2–3 NIV

"More time, Lord. I just need more time." Hezekiah turned his face to the wall—completely distracting himself from the things going on around him—and pleaded with God. "I've been faithful. I've been devoted. I've tried to live a good life. Please spare my life and give me more time to do the things I need to do."

Though Hezekiah wasn't sure what would happen next, the Lord heard his prayer and answered. He gave this very anxious man fifteen more years of life and health. Can you imagine the joy Hezekiah must have experienced to be given such a gift after thinking all was over?

Have you ever begged God for something? Have you been that desperate, so filled with

anxiety, that you had no choice but to turn your face away from the problem and plead with your heavenly Father for an answer to a problem you faced? Perhaps you weren't sure how the Lord would respond, but you had to try.

During those moments, anxiety can creep over you like a shroud. But God wants you to toss it off and increase your faith. Step one: Turn your face to the Waymaker. Step two: Ask in faith. Step three: Praise Him even if the answer doesn't come right away.

There's more life left in you. Don't give up. Turn your face to Him even now.

Lord, I won't give up. I will turn my face away from my problems and toward You, my Waymaker. You will make a way even when it feels impossible. Amen.

Single-ness

Yet the LORD longs to be gracious to you;
therefore he will rise up to show you
compassion. For the LORD is a God of justice.
Blessed are all who wait for him!
ISAIAH 30:18 NIV

"Am I going to be alone for the rest of my life?" "Will I always have to pay the bills by myself?" "Will anyone ever love me. . .for me?" Lindsey fretted over these questions not just occasionally but daily. In the still of the night, she reached her arm across the bed and rested her hand on the empty side. Maybe one day someone would occupy that space. . . . Until then, she was on her own. And she felt the loneliness weigh down on her like a stone.

If you're single, no doubt you've fretted over the same questions Lindsey asked. You've second-guessed yourself, wondered if you had value, or fretted over the financial part of being single. Maybe you even dreamed of having someone seated next to you on the sofa or curled

up next to you in bed. But it hasn't happened, at least not yet. And the worries about how long you can keep going alone are wearing you out.

Being single isn't easy. And there's plenty to worry about if you're prone to being anxious. But God always makes a way for those who love Him, and He's especially gracious to those who are going it alone. Remember, you're not really alone. Your Waymaker is right there with you. And He's so gracious and loving. He's surrounded you with friends and loved ones to do life with. He will help you make a way through this season. He will.

Lord, with You I'm never alone. You're so precious to me. I feel Your kindness and Your love when there's no one to reach out and touch. Thank You, my Waymaker, for caring so much. Amen.

Paul and Silas

After they had been severely flogged, they were thrown into prison, and the jailer was commanded to guard them carefully. When he received these orders, he put them in the inner cell and fastened their feet in the stocks.
ACTS 16:23–24 NIV

Paul and Silas were stripped and beaten for spreading the Gospel. Afterward, they were thrown in prison. Can you imagine being jailed for your faith? The jailer was given a command to keep a close eye on them. He put them in an inner cell, far away from any potential escape, not that they planned to go anywhere. These two were content to be wherever the Lord led them.

The guard wasn't counting on an earthquake! At midnight, as Paul and Silas were worshipping the Lord in song and prayer, an earthquake shook the place so violently that the men were loosened from their chains. They were free to run but chose to stay behind and minister to the guard, to share the story of a

Savior who could free the guard from the psychological and spiritual chains that bound him.

Maybe you've felt bound like Paul and Silas. You've convinced yourself that you'll never see outside of your proverbial prison walls. You've fretted and worried that nothing will ever change, that your situation is hopeless.

Take heart! If God could use an earthquake to rattle Paul and Silas's chains, think of what He'll do for you! You weren't meant to live in chains. Your Waymaker is intent on bringing you out from behind prison walls and setting you free.

Lord, thank You for setting me free from
the chains that have held me. I won't worry.
I won't fret. I'll trust You to shake the building
until I'm totally free. Amen.

Was It Something I Said?

He heals the brokenhearted
and binds up their wounds.
PSALM 147:3 ESV

"I wonder why they don't like me." "Is it something I said?" "Am I really so different that I'll never fit in?"

Maybe you've pondered these questions. You've looked at the cliques around you—women at church, neighbors, ladies at your child's school—and wondered how they so easily slip into units. They go out for coffee, swap stories about their kids, co-teach Bible studies. They squabble and make up, disagree over politics and then agree not to talk about it, and basically have normal relationships. They all seem so happy. . .and normal.

And you're beginning to worry you're not normal. You're never going to fit in. You're not the same in style, attitude, likes, and dislikes. They seem to walk right by you and not even notice you.

Here's some good news for you: God notices. He sees when you're overlooked, when you're feeling ostracized, and when your heart is broken. Better still, He cares. And God has already made a way out of these worries and concerns you've adopted as a result of your loneliness. He's invited you to be a friend with Him, to share your deepest wishes and dreams, and to pour out your heart when it's broken. What a precious Waymaker! And oh, how He loves you!

Don't fret! He has friends out there for you. Stop looking in the obvious places, and notice those who, like you, have felt left out. Perhaps you'll find that the friendliest of people were right there all along.

Thank You, Lord, for being the best
of friends, the kind who includes all.
I'm grateful to be in Your inner circle. Amen.

What Will the Neighbors Say?

*Jacob was the father of Joseph. Joseph was
the husband of Mary, and Mary was the
mother of Jesus. Jesus is called the Christ.*
MATTHEW 1:16 NCV

"Your fiancée is going to have a baby. And oh,
by the way. . .the Father is God, Himself."

Can you even imagine what Joseph must've
been thinking as he received this seemingly
unbelievable news from the angel Gabriel?
How shocked he must have been. Surely, he
questioned the validity of it all. Maybe he even
wondered if he'd heard correctly!

And yet, he followed through and did all he
was instructed to do. He took Mary privately and
treated her with the same love and respect. And
when the time came that she delivered Baby
Jesus, Joseph took Him as his own and raised
Him, even bringing Jesus up to be a carpenter
just like him.

No doubt Joseph worried about what others
thought of his situation with Mary. Likely, the

village gossips had a field day! Can't you just see them, gathered at the well, filling their buckets and each others' ears with chatter?

Maybe you've had similar worries. You've faced the "What will they think?" question.

Here's the truth: the only opinion that matters is God's. Even if you're caught in a trap of your own making, you can still count on the Lord to see you through it as long as you repent and turn to Him. So, don't fret over what others might be thinking or saying. Just stay focused on your Waymaker, and trust His plan to see you through.

*Lord, I trust You even when tongues are
wagging. I won't listen to them, Father.
Yours is the only voice that matters. Amen.*

Near to the Brokenhearted

*When the righteous cry for help,
the Lord hears and delivers them out of
all their troubles. The Lord is near to the
brokenhearted and saves the crushed in spirit.*
PSALM 34:17–18 ESV

Julie swung her legs over the edge of the examining table and sighed. She had just finished listing a litany of complaints to her doctor—everything from stomach issues to headaches. Now that the lengthy list was finally complete, she felt a bit like a hypochondriac. Would he see her as such? Instead of responding to her health woes, he gave her a sympathetic look.

"Tell me what's going on in your life," the doctor said.

A sigh escaped. Should she really open up this Pandora's box? Would he think she was crazy? "Well, I've recently separated from my husband, and I've been pretty unsure about the future."

"I'm not surprised to see the health problems creep up. It's not uncommon when you're

wound up with worry. Are you sleeping okay? Eating properly? Getting exercise?"

Another sigh followed from Julie. "There have been a lot of sleepless nights," she said after a moment. "And my diet has been off. I can't remember the last time I had a truly decent meal. I just nibble on this and that."

"Mm-hmm. Thought so," the doctor responded.

Maybe you've been there too. The breakup of a relationship has left your stomach in knots with physical ailments that were indescribable. It has affected you physically, mentally, and emotionally. Here's good news! Your Waymaker sees and already has a plan to get you to the other side of this valley you are walking through. Don't give up, and don't give in to despair.

Lord, sometimes I feel like I'm stuck. My situation has worn me down. But You are reminding me that I have a role to play in getting through this. I'll do my part, Father, and trust You with the rest. Amen.

Blessed Assurance

The Spirit himself bears witness with
our spirit that we are children of God.
ROMANS 8:16 ESV

Perhaps you've heard of Fanny Crosby, the great hymn writer. Her life was filled with ups and downs. A mistake at the hands of a medical quack caused her to go blind as an infant. What should have been a simple infection turned into a lifelong disability because of his negligence.

Some might have lashed out, angry at the doctor or filled with bitterness at her unfair plight. But not Fanny! Instead, she considered her blindness to be a blessing. Instead of complaining, instead of worrying about all of the things she couldn't do, she made up her mind to be usable to God, no matter what. In other words, bitterness never played a role in her life.

Fanny began to compose music and eventually wrote between 5,500 and 9,000 hymns, many of which are still sung today. Her legacy began with a mistake, a problem that would

have derailed someone of lesser courage. But it ended with a gift that has spread from generation to generation, inspiring and encouraging the masses.

Maybe you've struggled with things you consider unfair. You want to cry out, "Why me?" Instead of doing that and instead of living in a constant state of despair over your plight, turn it into praise like Fanny did. Throw away any traces of bitterness or anger. God—your great Waymaker—will see you through this. He adores you and wants the very best for you. Today, put your assurance, your confidence, in the One who is standing nearby, ready to make a way.

Lord, I won't worry about the unfairness of my life or the things that others have done to hurt me. Instead, I'll focus on You, my Waymaker, and trust You to turn my lemons into lemonade! Amen.

Even Now

Fear not, for I am with you; be not dismayed,
for I am your God; I will strengthen you,
I will help you, I will uphold you
with my righteous right hand.
ISAIAH 41:10 ESV

Lynn wrung her hands as she waited for the doctor to come into the room. For weeks she'd undergone test after test. What he was looking for, she could not say, but based on the sorts of tests he was running, Lynn feared the worst. And judging from the look on his face when he finally entered the room minutes later, her fears were well founded.

She sat stunned as he gave her his diagnosis —stomach cancer. Fear gripped her, but so did something else: understanding. Suddenly, it all made sense. . .the pain, the problematic symptoms, the inability to eat without getting sick. Lynn did her best to process the news as the doctor carried on about PET scans and treatments he'd like to start, but she found

herself twisted up inside. How could she possibly process all of this? And would she—could she—recover?

Maybe you've been in Lynn's shoes. Perhaps you sat in a doctor's office, awaiting news. And when it came, maybe you had an impossible time processing it, as Lynn did. Perhaps you also had a strange sense of relief, realizing you hadn't imagined all those symptoms. They made sense now in light of the diagnosis. But how will you move forward from here?

God wants you to know that He will make a way for you through whatever news you're facing. Yes, you're facing unseen obstacles. And yes, there will be moments when you're terrified. There are bound to be worries, but He will be right there, helping you focus on whatever steps you need to take. Trust Him. Even now.

Lord, I can't imagine how I'll take a step
forward after such bad news, but I will
do my best to keep my focus on You.
I'm counting on You, Father. Amen.

For Such a Time as This

"For if you keep silent at this time, relief and deliverance will rise for the Jews from another place, but you and your father's house will perish. And who knows whether you have not come to the kingdom for such a time as this?"

ESTHER 4:14 ESV

The fate of her people rested in her hands. Wow. Can you even imagine the stress Esther must have felt as she tried to run interference between the Jewish people and the king? No pressure, right? She kept her cool and did all that needed to be done. As a result of her willingness to remain focused on the Lord, her people were saved.

A lot can be accomplished when you're a willing servant. When you step out in faith, surprising even yourself, great things can and will happen.

Yes, there will be worries. Courage and fear go hand in hand, after all. And sure, there will be moments the pressure will get to you. But

when you offer yourself in service to the King of kings, remarkable things can happen. And, oh, the stories you'll have to tell after the fact!

Who are you standing in the gap for today? Who is on your "needs to be saved" list? Like Esther, you can keep standing, keep believing, keep trusting. And never forget: you were put here on Planet Earth at "such a time as this" so that you could impact the lives of those around you.

Lord, I won't fret when I'm standing in the gap for others. I won't look at circumstances. I'll just keep trusting You and reminding myself that You created me for this time, this season, and these people. Amen.

Great Things on the Horizon

"Let not your hearts be troubled.
Believe in God; believe also in me."

JOHN 14:1 ESV

"Pack up your desk and go."

Janelle stared at her boss, not sure she was fully understanding him. "You're. . .you're firing me?"

"Effective immediately. Get your things and clear out."

Nothing about this made sense. The accusation her coworker had made against her was false. Totally and completely false. Surely her boss would eventually see that. . .right?

In the meantime, how in the world could she go on paying her mortgage and taking care of her kids without an income? She stared at him in disbelief, hoping she'd somehow misunderstood; but judging from the tight expression on his face, she had not. He wanted her gone. . .now.

Janelle raced from his office, tears streaming. She couldn't think clearly but worked as

fast as she could to pack up and leave the office. How could she bear it? A cloak of grief and pain wrapped itself around her, twisting her heart and leaving her in anguish. "How, Lord? How will I survive? What will I do?"

It's hard to imagine that God can use any situation, even one like Janelle's, for good. But He can. There are great things on the horizon, no matter what you've been through. Your Way-maker can make a way to a newer, better job, one where employees are seen for who they really are. And in the meantime, He can and will make provision for those He adores.

Lord, I've been there. I've been scared that I wouldn't be able to cover the bills without my paycheck. But You've always provided, Father. I'm so grateful that You know exactly where I should be. . .and why. Amen.

Just in Time

And he said, "Jesus, remember me
when you come into your kingdom."
LUKE 23:42 ESV

The pain was unbearable. Agonizing. A life of thievery had led him here—to this cross where he now hung. Off in the distance, another thief was nailed to a tree and was writhing in pain. But all of the attention seemed to be on the man in the middle, the one the soldiers were just lifting into place.

Jesus. Who was this man, anyway? And why the big following?

The thief looked out over the crowd and tried to make sense of it all. Some of the people were weeping as if mourning Jesus' impending death. What would it feel like to have people adore you like that? Still others were mocking and tormenting. He certainly knew what that felt like.

Time passed, and the thief began to feel drawn to the man in the middle. Was He really

the Savior, as so many of His followers seemed to believe?

The thief suddenly felt the need to call out to Jesus. "Remember me when You come into Your kingdom."

Jesus' response startled him: "Today you will be with Me in paradise."

Wow! He didn't feel worthy, hadn't even lived a life dedicated to this man as so many of the others had done, and yet—just like that—everything changed.

Maybe you've been swept into the kingdom too and didn't feel worthy. You've worried that others will view your conversion as too convenient.

No worries allowed! God has made a way for you to be His, and His you are! How wonderful to be part of the kingdom. . .at last!

Lord, I'm so grateful You loved me enough to sweep me into the fold! I won't fret over what others think. I will simply celebrate being loved by You. Amen.

God's Battle Record

"For nothing will be impossible with God."
LUKE 1:37 ESV

How many battles do you win compared to those you lose? Some would call this your battle record. When you review your life, would you say you're more winner or loser? No doubt you've seen the good and the bad!

Did you realize that God has the best track record as a warrior? Every battle He wages, He wins. There's a victory every time as long as God is doing the fighting. Wow! Remarkable!

That knowledge should bring you great peace. Your track record doesn't matter. Even if you feel like a total loser, it's not your record you need to be concerned about. You can put your trust in His work, not your own.

Now that you realize He's the one in charge, how does that make you feel? Are you breathing a huge sigh of relief that you're not carrying the weight of the battle? The things that seemed impossible just moments ago are totally

possible now that they're in God's hands. And what a relief to know that His battle record is the best ever.

Whew! You don't have to worry. You don't have to take the pressure upon yourself. You can trust in the One who created you to take care of the things that matter—big and small. Failing is not a possibility when your Waymaker is the one in charge.

Lord, I trust You to take control. You have the best track record ever! You're a winner every time, Father. I'm so glad things are in Your hands, not mine. Amen.

When All Is Taken

*"Blessed is the man who trusts in the Lord,
whose trust is the Lord. He is like a tree planted
by water, that sends out its roots by the stream,
and does not fear when heat comes, for its leaves
remain green, and is not anxious in the year of
drought, for it does not cease to bear fruit."*
JEREMIAH 17:7–8 ESV

Job was a man of God who did everything right.
In spite of his upright living, the enemy swept
in and stole everything from him—his family,
his home, his cattle, his livelihood, even his
health. He reached such a low point that the
temptation to curse God and die became a very
real possibility.

But he didn't curse God, and he didn't die.
He remained steadfast, and in the end, God
restored everything he had lost.

Maybe you feel like Job. You've lost a lot.
You've wondered at times, *Where is God? Why
is He allowing all of these awful things to happen
to me?* You've worried (and rightfully so) that

things will continue to get worse before they get better.

When you reach that point, remember that God is in the restoration business. He truly will make a way through all your troubles. Your worries and concerns can't give way to despair. You have a Waymaker, and He adores you. He's going to restore you, and He'll do so in a way that brings joy to your heart and tears of relief to your eyes.

God, You are my restorer! What the enemy has stolen from me, You have given back. I've worried and fretted so much over my losses, Lord, but I'm reminded today that You will make a way even when it seems I'm at the end. Amen.

Our Great Provider

*"But seek first the kingdom of God and
his righteousness, and all these things
will be added to you. Therefore do not be
anxious about tomorrow, for tomorrow
will be anxious for itself. Sufficient
for the day is its own trouble."*

Matthew 6:33–34 esv

Penny stared inside the pantry at the near-empty shelves and tried to imagine how she could manage to make enough meals to see her family through the rest of the week. A couple of bags of pasta. Some tuna fish. A few cans of tomato sauce and a handful of other items. But how could she manage to turn these things into proper meals? The freezer was nearly bare as well. She simply didn't think she could manage.

Imagine her surprise, later that afternoon, when the doorbell rang and a neighbor stood outside. She held out a couple of plastic bags. "Hey, girl! My husband went to the meat market and came back with so much stuff I can't possibly squeeze it all into my freezer. Could you use

some hamburger and chuck roast? I have some extra chicken breasts too. Oh, and sausage. What do you think? Do you have room for it?"

Penny could hardly believe her ears. With tears in her eyes, she offered up a joyous, "Yes, thank you!"

Maybe you've been there. You've stared at a near-empty pantry and wondered how God could possibly stretch your dry goods into enough meals to feed the kids. But somehow—miraculously—He did. While you were fretting, God was already stretching loaves and fishes to meet your needs. He was making a way at the very moment you were fretting. What a good and gracious heavenly Father He is.

Lord, You are my provision. I don't need to worry about where the next meal will come from. I can trust You, my Waymaker! Amen.

Don't Run Away

But Jonah ran away from the Lord and
headed for Tarshish. He went down to Joppa,
where he found a ship bound for that port.
After paying the fare, he went aboard and
sailed for Tarshish to flee from the Lord.
JONAH 1:3 NIV

Have you ever been stressed out over something
the Lord asked you to do? Maybe He nudged at
your heart and asked you to apologize to someone for something you said, but you didn't want
to. Or maybe He wanted you to up your game at
the office, to give more of yourself. Ugh. Doing
so felt too stressful.

There are countless stories of people who
fretted over God's instructions to do hard
things, but no greater tale than Jonah's. The
Lord instructed him to go to Ninevah to tell the
people they needed to repent for their sins, but
Jonah didn't want to go. (Can you blame him?
It's tough to point out someone's sins to them,
after all!) So Jonah ran the other direction. It

wasn't until he was caught in the belly of the whale that he learned the hard lesson: it's better to do what God asks the first time.

Sure, there's a lot to worry about when it comes to stepping out in faith, but it sure beats getting trapped in the belly of a whale. Don't be a Jonah. Trust your Waymaker. If He's asking you to do something, He'll give you all you need to get through it. Remember, it's His power, not yours. His strength, not yours.

Grab your Waymaker's hand and run toward the situation, not away from it.

*Lord, I'm reaching for Your hand today.
I'll admit. . .I'm scared. But I know I can
trust You, my wonderful Waymaker. Amen.*

What's to Become of Us?

"For if you remain silent at this time, relief and deliverance for the Jews will arise from another place, but you and your father's family will perish. And who knows but that you have come to your royal position for such a time as this?"

ESTHER 4:14 NIV

Life on Planet Earth is changing so rapidly that it's difficult to keep up. Standards are changing. Morals are in a downward spiral. And sometimes it's hard not to get distressed about it all. Maybe you can't help but worry about what kind of world you'll be leaving behind for your children, grandchildren, and great-grandchildren. You wonder if they will be truth seekers or if they will succumb to the moral decline.

Think back to the story of Esther in the Bible. One of the key takeaways from that story is that she was born "for such a time as this." God doesn't make mistakes. He made sure you—and your kids—and their kids—were born

into the very time frame He chose. He didn't inadvertently plop you down in the twentieth or twenty-first century instead of placing you in the eighteenth century. It doesn't work like that.

You can trust God with His timing. No matter how rough things get (and it can get distressing, watching the news and seeing all of the chaos), be reminded that you are right here, right now because this is where He has placed you. He's going to give you—and those beautiful grandkids—courage and tenacity to face whatever obstacles the world might throw at you and them.

Lord, I trust You with my children and grandchildren, nieces and nephews. This world might be falling apart, but You're not. You can hold things together with just one word. I trust You, my Waymaker. Amen.

Staying Afloat

*By faith Noah, being warned by God concerning
events as yet unseen, in reverent fear constructed
an ark for the saving of his household. By this
he condemned the world and became an heir
of the righteousness that comes by faith.*

HEBREWS 11:7 ESV

Can you imagine what Noah must have been
thinking as the waters rose around the ark and
eventually lifted the vessel up, up, up to begin
floating? No one had ever built a boat before.
For that matter, no one had ever seen rain or
floodwaters. The very idea of an object floating
above the houses and trees below was unheard
of. Yet here he was, up above those who had lost
their lives, sailing like a seasoned pro atop the
floodwaters.

It's easy to imagine his terror, his gut-
twisting worries as that ark took off toward its
unnamed destination. Would the ship hold,
or would they eventually sink? Would God
really watch over them, making sure they had

everything they needed for the journey? How would he feed all those animals? How could he keep the ark from tipping over? What would happen when he got to dry land again? How could he and his family possibly start over?

You may have never floated on floodwaters on an ark, but no doubt you've faced spiritual floodwaters in your life. You've wondered if your proverbial ship would sink, drowning you in a moment's notice. It's hard not to be afraid or to worry when you can't see where you're heading.

Isn't it remarkable to think that your Way-maker knows exactly how your story will end? All He asks of you is that you trust Him while you're afloat. He can squelch any worries as long as you keep your eyes on Him.

Lord, I want to stay afloat, so I'll keep on trusting You even when I have no idea where my ship will land. I know You love me, Father, and want the best for me. How I love You! Amen.

The Worries of Aloneness

Turn to me and be gracious to me,
for I am lonely and afflicted.
PSALM 25:16 ESV

Shirley paced her living room. She paused to glance out the window as a car drove by. Overcome by boredom, she took a seat in her recliner and picked up her phone to check her email. Nothing but junk mail. She deleted it with a sigh. A quick scroll led her to her online social media account. She had a couple notifications but nothing from her family or friends. Everyone must be busy. Shirley set the phone down, leaned back in the chair, and closed her eyes, ready for a nap. For some reason, she found tears stinging her eyes.

Maybe you've spent some time in that recliner. You know the pain of loneliness. Maybe your spouse has passed on or your kids have flown the nest. Perhaps your best friend moved away or remarried, leaving you alone. You spend your days pacing, wondering what you can do

to occupy your time.

God hasn't forgotten you. Instead of fretting over your loneliness, give that pain to Him. Instead of plaguing yourself with questions like "Will I always be by myself?" shift your focus to the Lord and to those around you. God is going to make a way through the loneliness for you. Your Waymaker cares.

Sometimes the aloneness really gets to me, Lord. I don't know if I can handle all the worries associated with it. I'm grateful You never leave me, Father. Shift my focus to You and to those around me who might be hurting or in need of care. Make me outward-focused, I pray. Amen.

Known by Those around You

In the sixth month of Elizabeth's pregnancy,
God sent the angel Gabriel to Nazareth,
a town in Galilee, to a virgin pledged to be
married to a man named Joseph, a descendant
of David. The virgin's name was Mary.

LUKE 1:26–27 NIV

The virgin's name was Mary.

We can deduce a lot from just that one sentence. First, this young woman was pure, hence the term *virgin*. She had never been with a man. Second, she was known by her name—Mary—which means that people in her village knew exactly who she was.

In some ways, being known by everyone in the village was a blessing. Maybe you've lived in a small town where everyone knew you by name, or perhaps you attend a church where you're all closely bonded like that. Everyone knows everyone.

But there are some downfalls to being known by so many. If you mess up, even a little,

everyone knows it. Mary didn't mess up (obviously), but no doubt her situation tarnished her reputation.

Maybe your reputation has been tarnished too. Your group knows all the details. Because you're known to them, you've been unable to hide the ugly realities.

Aren't you glad you don't have to? God can take even the most humbling situation—even the things you are ashamed of—and turn them around. Your Waymaker can make a way for you out of any embarrassment to a brand-new beginning.

Lord, I'm glad I'm known by those who love me. And I'm grateful for the many times they've walked me through rough seasons, some brought on by my own actions. I don't know how You keep making a way for me, especially when I self-sabotage, but You love me so much that You do. I'm eternally grateful. Amen.

The Rainbow Baby

*Now faith is the assurance of things hoped for,
the conviction of things not seen.*

<small>HEBREWS 11:1 ESV</small>

Alexis was tickled pink to receive the news that she was expecting, but she couldn't stop the nagging fears that this pregnancy might end the way the last one had. Losing her baby boy in the fourth month had been devastating. She couldn't go through that again. She just couldn't.

Much to her relief, the pregnancy moved along beautifully, and she gave birth to a six-pound baby girl right on schedule. Only when she looked into those beautiful, wide eyes did she finally breathe a sigh of relief. Her rainbow baby (a term given to a healthy baby born after the loss of a child) was absolutely perfect.

Maybe you've been in Alexis' shoes. Perhaps you lost a baby either through miscarriage or stillbirth. You wonder if you'll ever have a rainbow baby. Then you find out you're

expecting, but you can't calm down. You can't stop worrying.

Your Waymaker wants to meet you in the middle of your worries. He longs to take your fears, your concerns, your grief and carry those things close to His heart. He will make a way for you to see your dreams fulfilled. The picture might not look like you expected, but God knows just how to place people into families.

Trust Him even if you've faced a cataclysmic loss. The Lord will truly make a way to fill that void in your heart. . .even if it seems impossible.

Lord, I've been brokenhearted before and can't face it again. The fear is huge when I think about another loss. But I trust You, my precious Waymaker. Keep me strong and faith-filled, I pray. Amen.

Sharing the Good News

He said to them, "Go into all the world
and preach the gospel to all creation."
MARK 16:15 NIV

If you've studied the Wesley brothers (John and Charles), you know that they had a passion for sharing their testimonies with as many people as they could reach. These two men traveled on horseback from place to place and were filled with zeal to get the word out about the saving love and grace of Jesus.

John was an amazing and powerful preacher. He traveled an average of eight thousand miles per year. Can you imagine? He went on to become one of the most beloved men in England.

Maybe you hear this story and cringe at the notion of having to spread the Gospel. You find it difficult to talk to others, especially your coworkers, neighbors, and friends, about your faith. It's not always easy, especially in this current culture. Many people are self-focused and don't want to turn their eyes to the Lord.

Instead of fretting over whether or not you're doing a good job spreading the Gospel, just ask the Lord to give you the courage to enter into a quiet conversation with one person—in a way that's not uncomfortable or weird. It could be as easy as saying, "I'll be praying for you," to a coworker who's ill or taking a meal to an elderly person who lives alone. Perhaps you could simply share your testimony, the story of what the Lord has done in your life.

God can open doors of conversation in the most natural and wonderful way. Your Way-maker is an amazing door opener after all!

Lord, I trust You to open doors of conversation with people who need to know You. Give me courage, and show me how to share Your heart with those I meet. Amen.

Losing Religious Freedoms

The fear of man lays a snare,
but whoever trusts in the LORD is safe.
PROVERBS 29:25 ESV

We live in an interesting day and age, when it's not always easy to stand up for your faith. Perhaps you hold certain biblical principles near and dear to your heart, but your ideology isn't popular in the current culture. In fact, you've come under fire for stating your beliefs.

We know that in the last days, it's going to get harder and harder to stand strong and not bow to the winds of the adversary. You can do it. Even if you feel like you just want to clam up and not let others know the truth of the Gospel, God will make a way if you trust Him.

It's critical that all believers pray for their leaders—from the local leaders all the way up to those in the highest offices of the land. If God's people will pray and humble themselves, He promises to heal their land. The body of Christ must come together, especially now, and pray

as never before. We should kneel to ask God to forgive us for our personal sins and the sins of our nation.

There may come a day when we have no religious freedoms at all. It's terrifying to think of. We could be like the apostles in days of old, jailed for our faith. But even then, our Waymaker will make a way. So don't give in to fear. If God could take care of Paul, Timothy, Silas, Peter, and the other great men of faith, He can certainly make a way for you.

*Lord, I will do my best to stand strong.
I won't let fear or worry cripple me as I
see what's going on around me. I'll
trust You to see me through. Amen.*

A Name Change

*Then Abram bowed facedown on the ground.
God said to him, "I am making my agreement
with you: I will make you the father of many
nations. I am changing your name from
Abram to Abraham because I am making
you a father of many nations."*
GENESIS 17:3–5 NCV

Do you ever wish you could just change your name, move to a new place, and start over? A tropical island sounds good right about now, doesn't it? Maybe you've messed up something so badly that you'd like to run and hide in a cave. Or maybe your spouse has done something really awful and landed himself in jail. Everyone knows. . .and you're so ashamed. Hiding in a cave might be a desirable option.

Here's the truth—you can begin again. No matter how bad the mistake, God can truly offer forgiveness and a fresh start.

Acknowledge your mistakes, yes. Go to those you've wronged and ask for forgiveness.

That's the biblical thing to do. Repent to the Lord and ask for His forgiveness. He will offer it freely.

Once those things are done, place it in the hands of your Waymaker. Don't worry. Don't fret. Don't get wound up, thinking about how it would be easier to run. Instead, walk it out, one step at a time.

God will take this once-messy situation and use it for good. He's the best at doing that! Accept the new you, the one with the new name—Forgiven!—and move forward with hope.

Lord, I'm so grateful for my new name.
You've taken my icky past and washed it clean.
Now I can stand with confidence, ready to
begin again, a new child. Forgiven. Amen.

More than Potential

I can do all things through
him who strengthens me.
PHILIPPIANS 4:13 ESV

You don't feel up to par. You certainly don't feel you measure up to your coworkers, and sometimes you wonder if you ever will. Everyone says you're loaded with potential, but you don't want potential. You want outcomes. Now.

You really give it your all, but your boss doesn't seem to see your talents and abilities, and you're beginning to doubt them too. Maybe you'll just be known as "the one who had potential" forever. Or maybe, in a fit of despair, you've wondered if you should consider a completely different line of work.

But you decide to hang on, and with a heavenly nudge, you begin to morph and grow. Your doubts, worries, and concerns begin to fade as progress is made and others see your growth.

Even in the toughest work situations, your Waymaker wants to see you excel. There's no

point in worrying about all the ways you don't measure up. Do the work that needs to be done, develop your skills as much as you can, and leave the rest to the Lord.

Is He capable? Do you really believe that? If so, then trust Him to fill in the gap and do what you—in and of yourself—cannot. With God's hand in yours, you have more than potential. You're really going places! You really can do all things through the One who gives you strength. Don't ever doubt it.

Lord, I'll admit I fall short. . .a lot. But You never fall short! You can take a vessel like me—one with flaws and shortcomings— and use her anyway. I'm so blessed and honored, Father! Amen.

From Mourning to Laughter

Then the LORD said, "I will certainly return to you about this time a year from now. At that time your wife Sarah will have a son." Sarah was listening at the entrance of the tent which was behind him. Abraham and Sarah were very old. Since Sarah was past the age when women normally have children, she laughed to herself, "My husband and I are too old to have a baby."
GENESIS 18:10–12 NCV

If you've known the pain of infertility, surely you can relate to Sarah's struggle. She had waited a long, long time to receive the news that a baby was on the way. The years had aged her beyond the point where most women could become pregnant. So, imagine her surprise when the Lord spoke through three strangers to tell her husband that she was going to give birth within the year.

"I'm too old for that now!" she said. . .and then laughed. What a joke, to think that an old woman could conceive and bear a child. Were

these men just being cruel?

Lo and behold, she did conceive and bear a child—a boy they named Isaac. Sarah named him "one who laughs" because the notion of getting pregnant at her age had given her the giggles.

Maybe you're not laughing right now. You're reading this and saying, "Lord, I want a child. And I don't want to wait until I'm really old. I'd prefer You answer my prayer. . .now." Like Sarah, you're reaching the giving-up point. There's no way to know exactly how your story will end, but consider what the Bible says in Genesis 21:1 (NIV): "Now the LORD was gracious to Sarah as he had said, and the LORD did for Sarah what he had promised."

He will be gracious to you too. How He fills that spot in your arms and heart will be up to Him, but your Waymaker will prove Himself faithful one way or another.

Lord, there are times when I'm heartbroken and wounded. I truly don't feel like laughing. But You are my great healer, and I trust You to turn hard seasons around. Amen.

A Healthy Mind and Heart

"Come to me, all who labor and are heavy laden, and I will give you rest. Take my yoke upon you, and learn from me, for I am gentle and lowly in heart, and you will find rest for your souls. For my yoke is easy, and my burden is light."
MATTHEW 11:28–30 ESV

Many people (even those inside the body of Christ) struggle with mental illness. As believers, it does no good to close our eyes to the problem and say it doesn't exist. There are genuine struggles faced by loving, godly people, and they need our encouragement and support. Many of them end up in a psychologist's office or visiting a psychiatrist for counsel and meds.

Maybe you're one of those people. You've worried yourself sick over the challenges going on in your heart and mind, and so you've finally decided to take action. You recognize the spiritual aspect of it (there is a very real enemy out there, and he loves to steal, kill, and destroy), but you're also aware of the fact that the medical

community has the ability to help.

It might seem difficult to believe when you're in the heat of the mental battle, but your Waymaker has a way through all things, even something as complicated and challenging as this.

Take comfort in this: You can trust Him with your mind. You can trust Him with your mental health. You can trust Him to make a way through the fog of chaos between your ears. He longs for you to be healed and whole. So don't give in to fear. Don't let worry keep you paralyzed. Instead, be set free and walk in new life with the hand of your heavenly Father clasped in yours.

Lord, I've had struggles. They've been hard to admit to others. I've battled depression or anxiety. I've faced even bigger challenges at times but was ashamed to admit it. Thank You for making a way even through the mental challenges, Father. Amen.

Rebuilding the Walls

"Let your ear be attentive and your eyes open, to hear the prayer of your servant that I now pray before you day and night for the people of Israel your servants, confessing the sins of the people of Israel, which we have sinned against you. Even I and my father's house have sinned."

NEHEMIAH 1:6 ESV

Nehemiah was emotionally shattered over the condition of the walls that lay in ruins around Jerusalem. He longed for them to be restored but knew it would take a lot of work. So, he rallied the troops. He gathered his friends, his people, and his strongest workers then dove in headfirst. He could've spent time worrying over his enemies, those who didn't want to see the walls rebuilt, but he laid those worries aside and got right to it.

There are things you're trying to rebuild in your life too. Friendships. Finances. Your faith. Your health. Your family. These things once lay in ruins, perhaps as a result of your own doing

or maybe at the hands of others. But you're ready. You're rolling up your sleeves and diving back in. You're rallying the troops and asking for their help to get the job done.

One thing you're not doing is worrying. It does no good. Walls aren't rebuilt of worries. So, lay them aside, and trust your Waymaker to be the foundation as you build. As much as you long for restoration, He wants it even more. And God is in the business of rebuilding, so you can trust Him every step of the way.

My great Waymaker, I need You!
There are broken-down places in my life—
in relationships, in my heart, in my faith.
You're the great rebuilder, the restorer of
all things. Today I choose to put my
trust in You, Father. Amen.

Fitting In

Humble yourselves, therefore, under the mighty hand of God so that at the proper time he may exalt you, casting all your anxieties on him, because he cares for you.

1 Peter 5:6–7 esv

It started in junior high. Linda didn't seem to fit in with the other girls. They were frilly, she was a tomboy. They huddled together to talk about makeup and hair. She simply wasn't interested in those things. They loved to talk about the boys they had crushes on. She was more content to play ball with the boys.

Things escalated in high school. Linda latched on to one clique of girls but found herself having to go to extraordinary measures to stay in their circle. As long as she played the role of grunt or gopher, they kept her in. But she started to feel superfluous. After a while, she just slipped away, happier to be on her own and more at ease in her own skin.

Maybe you've struggled to fit in with the

women around you too. You gaze at your reflection in the mirror and just feel different. You look different. Your interests are different. You simply don't fit. And that worries you. Shouldn't you have a circle of friends like others do?

God doesn't want you to fret over fitting in, and He certainly doesn't want you to go out of your way to force a fit. He has the right group of friends out there for you. And they're looking for you right now, just like you're looking for them. Trust your Waymaker to draw the perfect friends to your side. And don't be surprised if they don't look or act like the people you've known in the past. God has an amazing sense of humor and wants to surprise you.

Lord, I'm on the lookout for good friends,
those I can trust. I trust You with the process.
You are the Waymaker after all. You can certainly
bring them my way as You choose! Amen.

Over the Walls

When the LORD began to speak through
Hosea, the LORD said to him, "Go, marry a
promiscuous woman and have children
with her, for like an adulterous wife this land
is guilty of unfaithfulness to the LORD." So he
married Gomer daughter of Diblaim, and
she conceived and bore him a son.
HOSEA 1:2–3 NIV

The story of Hosea is quite heartbreaking. This godly man was instructed by God to marry a woman of the night. Gomer came into the marriage willingly but wanted *out* more than she had ever wanted *in*. According to the biblical story, she looked at the walls around her home as obstacles not protection. She eventually jumped the walls and took off to find a more exciting life on the outside.

Hosea responded by pursuing her time and time again. She jumped. He pursued. She jumped again. He pursued again. Gomer finally reached the point where she was completely

untouchable. . .or so she thought. She was in the depths of her despair, and Hosea reached out and gathered her in his arms. Where did he take her? Home, of course.

Perhaps you've felt like Gomer at times. You've gone in search of a more exciting life. Maybe you found yourself completely lost, feeling dirty and untouchable. You worried that God wouldn't take you back. Your Waymaker never stops chasing you, no matter how fast or far you run. It's His greatest desire to restore us fully. He makes a way back to His arms even when we're absolutely sure there's no way.

What's keeping you? Run home today!

Lord, I know how adventurous the world can seem. I've jumped over plenty of walls to get a closer look. But here I am, ready to admit that life with You is more fulfilling. Take me back, I pray. Amen.

Unnecessary Worry

"And which of you by being anxious can add a single hour to his span of life?"
MATTHEW 6:27 ESV

❧❧❧❧❧

Geri lived in fear of her loved ones passing away. The idea that one of them might precede her in death was terrifying. Sometimes, late at night, she would lie in her bed and visualize the loss of her mother. Or her son. Or her husband. She couldn't seem to shake the notion that those she loved would—or could—possibly die and leave her alone to grieve their loss. How could she go on living without the ones she loved? It seemed impossible.

It wasn't until someone she loved actually did pass away that she began to understand. Her father's transition to heaven was difficult, of course, but Geri found it strangely comforting to know that he was no longer struggling with diabetes. He was in heaven, completely healed and whole. This knowledge gave her the courage to face her fears. Heaven was the ultimate

victory, after all. And she would see her loved ones together again in a place where there was no pain or sorrow.

What about you? Have you mourned the loss of people who aren't even gone yet? Is your stomach knotted in fear as you think that one day they might be gone? Does fear make you think you couldn't possibly go on after losing someone you care about?

Instead of hyper-focusing on the pain those images present, shift your thinking. Ask your Waymaker for an eternal perspective. He will surely give it. And He will bring you peace in the process.

Lord, I don't want to mourn those who aren't even gone, and I sure don't want to live in fear. Give me Your thoughts, Your mind, and Your perspective, I pray. Amen.

Out of the Way

Preach the word; be prepared in season and out of season; correct, rebuke and encourage—with great patience and careful instruction.
2 Timothy 4:2 NIV

Has God ever gone out of His way to reach you?

Carrie was headed to the coffee shop to meet her friend. She was running late, and time was of the essence. Suddenly, she felt an odd nudge to stop and pick up a couple of grocery items for dinner. Can you imagine—late for a meeting and stopping to get groceries first?

Still, Carrie couldn't shake the feeling that God was prompting her, so she texted her friend to say she'd be a few minutes late and made a quick stop at the grocery store. A few minutes later, standing in the checkout line, the woman ahead of her seemed to be upset. She had tears in her eyes. Carrie garnered the courage to reach out to her and before long was praying for her.

Remarkable, how that works. . .right? What if Carrie hadn't listened to God? What if she

had chosen not to respond? Her response was correct, and God used her to speak a word of life to a total stranger and to pray in faith when the woman really needed the encouragement.

Our Waymaker will go to *any* length to encourage His children. . .even if it appears to interfere with our plans or send us out of our way. Has He ever used you like that? Isn't it wonderful to hear His still, small voice and then obey?

Lord, You are a Waymaker even if it means sending me out of my way. I'll go where You instruct, Father! I'm waiting for divine appointments even now. Amen.

Trust Him with Today

*"Peace I leave with you; my peace I give
to you. Not as the world gives do I give
to you. Let not your hearts be troubled,
neither let them be afraid."*

JOHN 14:27 ESV

Joanna was a worrier. As a child, her parents struggled with responsibility. She lived in a filthy house—difficult to navigate due to hoarding—and accidents often happened due to neglect. To make matters worse, her father's unwillingness to keep a job led to utilities being shut off. . .a lot. She learned to make do, to live in an alternate reality in her own mind. But even as an adult, she always feared the worst. At any moment, the rug would be pulled out from under them. She and her husband would lose their home. Their car would break down on the side of the road. Her children would have to go without.

As a result of this fear, she began to over-compensate. She became obsessive about

hoarding food. And clothes. And cleaning supplies. She purchased as much as she could on the off chance that she would one day be unable to care for her family.

Maybe you've been there. You lived in fear of having the rug pulled out from under you, so you stocked up. And stocked up. And stocked up some more. No doubt you can relate to Joanna's desire to tend to her family's needs even in a nonsensical way. Today, release those fears to the Lord. He'll make a way for you out of the fear and pain from the past. You can trust Him with today. He's not looking for a way to pull the rug out from under you.

Lord, I've been through some things in my life. They've turned me into the person I am now. But I don't have to stay stuck in the past, trapped by the fears of yesterday. I can trust You today, my Waymaker. How blessed I am. Amen.

A Different Point of View

*I do not hide your goodness in my heart; I
speak about your loyalty and salvation.
I do not hide your love and truth from
the people in the great meeting.*

PSALM 40:10 NCV

Imagine a world where everyone agreed with everyone else. Sounds lovely but also a little boring. Vibrant conversations make things interesting, and differing points of view are healthy. They keep us alert and thinking.

Maybe you don't like feeling different. Perhaps you have different political views from the rest of your family, or maybe you can't ever seem to agree with your friends on who you should vote for. They make it difficult for you, pointing fingers and accusing you of not seeing the light. They try to "educate" you. They hammer home their points until you're weary.

And that worries you. In fact, it worries you so much that you find yourself wondering if you should vote at all. They'll hound you if you do,

but you'll feel guilty if you don't.

Being different isn't a bad thing! Better to be one of a kind than to follow the masses without educating yourself. So study! Learn what needs to be learned. Make the political decisions you feel led to make based on your research and your quiet time with God. And don't let anyone drag you into a fight about it, especially on social media. It's hard to apologize for words spoken in haste in front of the whole world.

Go ahead. Be yourself. Vote your conscience. But love your fellow human being in the process.

I really do need Your help navigating this one, Lord! It's not easy to be the only one in a crowd with a different point of view. I want to stand for You, Father. Give me courage, strength, and most of all love for those who are different. Amen.

Grieving the Loss of a Friend

For I consider that the sufferings of this
present time are not worth comparing
with the glory that is to be revealed to us.
ROMANS 8:18 ESV

Tina and Deborah met in fourth grade and remained best friends all their lives. They grew up as neighbors, double-dated to prom, served as maid of honor at each other's weddings. They were there for each other as their children were born and cared about every trial.

When Deborah turned forty-six, she began to experience health issues. She was diagnosed with heart disease a few months into her struggles and eventually went on the heart transplant list. Tina never gave up believing that her best friend would be okay. But when Deborah passed away from complications after the transplant, it was more than Tina could take. She retreated, pulling away from family and other friends. How could God be so cruel to take the friend who meant the most to her?

She struggled with her emotions and her faith. She couldn't picture her world without Deborah in it. Over a period of months, she gave herself over to the grief. She ate the wrong foods, stopped visiting with people she loved, and even stopped caring about the quality of her work when on the job.

Maybe you've lost a friend too. Perhaps you've been frozen in place ever since. Today, your Waymaker wants to show you a way out of that fog to new life. Your friend wouldn't want you to grieve as unto death, and neither does the Lord. There are amazing days ahead.

Lord, I need You. My heart is so broken at my loss. I miss my friend so much. I would give anything to have her back. I'm so grateful we'll see each other again in heaven. Until then, please make a way out of this deep grief, I pray. Amen.

The Little Things

"Ask, and it will be given to you; seek, and you will find; knock, and it will be opened to you."
MATTHEW 7:7 ESV

Patti wasn't asking for much. She needed a rental home with its own washer and dryer in the unit. With a newborn and a toddler, she knew that carrying baskets of clothes to a laundry room wouldn't be practical. But as a single mom, she had limited resources. Very limited. In fact, her situation seemed downright impossible.

Instead of fretting, she decided to pray. She shared her heart and asked the Lord to meet her at her point of need, and God answered her prayers. A couple in her church owned a rental townhouse across the street from the church, and it was vacant. They offered to lower the price to help her out. Best of all, it came with a washer and dryer! It might seem like a little thing to some, but to Patti it was huge!

Maybe you've been blessed by "the little

things" too. Think of the many, many times God has made sure the finer points were taken care of. That time you found a twenty-dollar bill in a pocket of your purse. That time you realized you had food in the pantry you'd forgotten about. That time you almost ran out of gas. . .but didn't.

God can make a way. . .and put a smile on your face while He's doing it. He's in the details, for sure, and loves to delight you with His little surprises.

I'm so glad You care about the little things, Lord! You really do love to bless me, bringing delightful surprises along the way. I can trust You, my Waymaker, with all things large and small. How grateful I am! Amen.

Supernatural Provision

Trust in the LORD with all your heart,
and do not lean on your own understanding.
In all your ways acknowledge him, and he
will make straight your paths.
PROVERBS 3:5–6 ESV

Anne and her husband lived on the edge, financially speaking. She was a stay-at-home mom who homeschooled her children. He worked as a police officer, but his income wasn't really enough to sustain them, so he picked up extra jobs as they became available. To supplement their living, she started writing magazine articles for Christian publications.

Still, they found themselves juggling bills. Sometimes she would rob Peter to pay Paul. She'd cover all the utilities and plead with the mortgage company to roll back a payment. Sometimes that tactic would work, but at one point she found herself owing two mortgage payments at once and was short by three hundred dollars. She didn't tell a soul other than

her husband. She prayed about it and did her best to trust God.

She attended a Wednesday night prayer service at her church. Afterward, as she went to get her children from the nursery, a woman approached her. She extended her hand and said, "Anne, I don't know how to explain this, but this morning when I was praying, God put your face in front of me and said, 'Give this woman three hundred dollars.'"

Anne was shocked into complete silence. There was truly no way this woman could have known, short of a miracle from on high.

Maybe you've witnessed miracles like this in your life too. Your precious Waymaker gave you exactly what you needed when you needed it. Oh, how He loves you! And how He longs to meet every single need.

Lord, if You can give that woman three hundred dollars out of the blue, I know I can trust You to meet my needs. I won't fret. I'll trust You, my Waymaker. Amen.

Wishing and Wanting

*"Do not lay up for yourselves treasures on
earth, where moth and rust destroy and
where thieves break in and steal, but lay up
for yourselves treasures in heaven, where
neither moth nor rust destroys and where
thieves do not break in and steal. For where
your treasure is, there your heart will be also."*
MATTHEW 6:19–21 ESV

Bella looked around her picture-perfect house
and smiled. Everything was as she had always
dreamed it would be—a lovely home filled with
beautiful, stylish items. Two top-of-the-line
vehicles in the driveway. Kids in private school.
Terrific husband. Trips to the Bahamas. She was
living the dream, just as she'd always hoped.

But inside, something kept nagging at her.
How could they keep this up? Her husband
was great, but he struggled to be the primary
breadwinner. Her job at an accountant's office
was adequate, but she always felt the need to
earn more, to be more, to achieve more. Want,

want, want. Wish. Wish. Wish. Nothing was ever quite enough.

Maybe you're an overachiever too. You want the best of everything. You want people to look at your life and say, "She's a success!"

Living like that might sound fun, but it's difficult to maintain near-perfection. Instead of fretting over what you have or don't have (with material possessions or jobs), release your hold and ask God, "What's Your best for me?" He's your Waymaker. He has a plan for your best. He won't let you down. So, trust Him to make a way even if the outcome doesn't match the image of perfection in your head.

Lord, I love nice things but not at the expense of
my health and sanity. You are my provider.
I know You'll meet my needs. Help me to
curb my wants, I pray. Amen.

Job Shifts

*"Be strong and courageous. Do not fear
or be in dread of them, for it is the Lord
your God who goes with you. He will
not leave you or forsake you."*

Deuteronomy 31:6 esv

It started with a shift from one department to another within the company she worked for. Then Gloria lost her job altogether. So, she found another job at a similar company. That job lasted for a couple years, and then, due to the downturn of the economy, she was laid off. She couldn't really blame them. The last to be hired were always the first to be let go. Gloria considered herself fortunate enough to land another job, this time in a completely different field. After a while, she felt a bit like a yo-yo, bouncing from one place to the other.

Maybe you've bounced around too. You started at one company but ended up at another. You started with one type of work and ended up doing something else entirely. Sometimes

the craziness of it all can bring you a great deal of worry and discomfort. You find yourself questioning. . .everything. And the instability you feel is uncomfortable at best.

Even in the midst of the chaos, God is still in control. He's still your Waymaker, and He knows exactly where you are and where you're going. Doesn't that bring you an amazing sense of relief? He sees all of it, even when you're in a fog. So, trust Him in that fog. Do your best where you've landed, but be open to what's coming next. He has this. He will place your feet on solid ground when you keep your focus on Him.

Solid ground! That's what I need, Lord. I want to sit at Your feet, completely unshaken. . .even when everything around me is whirling. I trust You even in the midst of shifting seasons. Amen.

The Faith of Stephen

But Stephen, full of the Holy Spirit, looked up
to heaven and saw the glory of God, and Jesus
standing at the right hand of God. "Look," he
said, "I see heaven open and the Son of Man
standing at the right hand of God."
ACTS 7:55–56 NIV

If you've read the story of Stephen (found in
Acts 7), you know that this precious, godly man
had remarkable faith. He was found guilty of
spreading the Gospel. His punishment? Death.
Somehow, even as his oppressors surrounded
him, he saw a way out. Stephen, full of the Holy
Spirit, looked up. And when he did, do you
know what he saw? The glory of God. He also
saw Jesus, standing at the right hand of God.

We have so many lessons to learn from
Stephen's journey. There are things in this
life we're absolutely sure we can't survive—the
loss of a child, the death of a dream, the end-
ing of a marriage. And yet, if we have the faith
of Stephen, if we can just look up even in the

middle of the crisis, our Waymaker is right there, within sight. He's more keenly aware of what we're going through than we are! And He cares.

Do you believe God cares about where you are? Do you think He's already making a way to see you through? You can trust Him even when everything around you appears to be crumbling. Don't give up. Just *look* up.

Lord, I'm looking up today. Way up!
I'm shifting my gaze from the situation
around me to You, my Waymaker. My struggles
are great, but I've never come under the kind
of persecution Stephen suffered. I'll do my best
to keep things in perspective, Father. Amen.

Moving Woes

The LORD is my shepherd; I shall not want.
He makes me lie down in green pastures.
He leads me beside still waters.
PSALM 23:1–2 ESV

Kandi knew when she married a man in the military that she would be moving a lot. They would spend a couple years in one state, and then he'd be transferred to another. When active duty called, she would stay put with the kids until he returned, at which point there was usually another move. A part of her loved the adventure of it all, but when the kids began to complain that they couldn't make friends in the new places, it started to affect her. She began to worry about their academic progress, about their socialization, and even about her own friendships (or lack thereof).

Maybe you've moved around a lot too. You struggled to pay the rent, so you moved to a cheaper place. You went through a marital breakup and had to sell the house. Your

employer transferred you to another state. You've tried to find a good church, but with so many shifts, it seems impossible.

Moving is a part of life, but there are plenty of worries associated with packing everything up and beginning again. God doesn't want you to fret over all that. He's created a path for you that's filled with joy and peace. You can trust Him to make a way even when you're shifting from location to location. If you truly place your trust in God, your Waymaker, you'll see that these moves really can be an adventure.

Lord, I want to see my life as an adventure. I'll trust You to work out the details with every move I make, Father. Amen.

David and Goliath

*David said to the Philistine, "You come against
me with sword and spear and javelin, but I
come against you in the name of the LORD
Almighty, the God of the armies of Israel,
whom you have defied."*
1 SAMUEL 17:45 NIV

The small business squaring off with the major
corporation. The tiny girl standing face-to-face
with a bully. The Christian taking a stand for
her faith in spite of the political correctness of
the day. There are plenty of David and Goliath
situations out there. Movies glorify them, books
share their tales, and you love watching the little
guy win over the bully.

So what do you do when you feel like David?
Do your knees knock? Are you consumed by
worry and fear? Do you turn and run, convinced
Goliath will take you down? Or do you stand your
ground and reach for your slingshot?

Here's the truth: God is your Waymaker even
when you're facing Goliath. Sure, your knees

are knocking, but that's okay! He made a way for young David, and He'll make a way for you. Don't let your fear of the giant rob you of your faith that God is bigger. . .and stronger.

He will make a way. No matter what you're facing today. No matter how the enemy taunts you. No matter how massive the problem or how tiny you feel. God has already crafted a way for that giant to fall and for you to have the victory.

Lord, I have faced many Goliaths in my life. They've terrified me! But I'm reminded today that they are nothing for You, my Waymaker. You can take them down in no time. I'm trusting You to do just that. Amen.

Those Pesky Medical Bills

*And my God will supply every need of yours
according to his riches in glory in Christ Jesus.*
PHILIPPIANS 4:19 ESV

Darla's job didn't provide medical insurance,
so she was forced to buy an individual policy,
which ended up costing a fortune. She had to
take a policy with a high deductible; otherwise,
the cost would be beyond her reach. So, when
she ended up in the hospital with pneumonia,
there was a big bill to pay at the end. A six-
thousand-dollar deductible, to be precise,
along with 20 percent of the rest of the bill.

She didn't have that kind of money sitting in
an account somewhere, so, after she recovered,
Darla had to take on extra work just to pay the
bill. It took some doing, but with God's help, the
hospital eventually cut a deal with her, whittling
down the total to a more manageable amount.

Likely you've faced medical bills at some
point too. They can seem overwhelming, and
you often feel like tiny David facing the giant,

Goliath. Remember, God sees all. He knows what you're facing. Don't be surprised if He uses friends, loved ones, your church, or even family members to help you during seasons like this. Your Waymaker loves you, and His people adore you too.

Lord, I don't know how You do it, but You always manage to make a way even when I'm facing a season of financial struggles. Thank You for the many times You've met my need, Father. Amen.

Unexpected Financial Losses

And my God will supply every need of yours according to his riches in glory in Christ Jesus.
PHILIPPIANS 4:19 ESV

Perhaps you've heard people use the expression "The bottom fell out." You'll usually hear that after someone has lost a home or a job or has suffered a great financial loss. We usually can't predict financial losses. That's why so many of them are called "unexpected" losses. Stock market crashes, savings lost to medical bills, putting all of your savings into the care of an elderly parent. These things can leave you stunned and devastated, often frozen in place.

When the bottom does fall out, you have two options: give in to fear and despair or continue to trust God as if He knows all. Which choice do you make? It's easy to say, "Oh, I'm sure my faith would remain intact if the stock market fell," but it's another thing to live it out.

Here's the truth: worrying does no good. If anything, it depletes you of your strength and

shifts your focus to the problem rather than to God. He longs for you to trust in Him even in the middle of the worst-case scenario. Foreclosure. Job loss. Broken-down car. He's big enough to handle any or all of those. He will make a way. Even as you're staring at the steam billowing from under the hood of your SUV, He has a plan to take care of you.

Lord, these big, catastrophic things are terrifying. Huge medical bills. Losing my savings. Losing my home. How I worry and fret. But I can trust You, my Waymaker, even when the bottom falls out. You're consistently good even when my situation looks dire. How I love You for making a way. Amen.

A Babble of Voices

*And let the peace of Christ rule in
your hearts, to which indeed you were
called in one body. And be thankful.*
COLOSSIANS 3:15 ESV

If you've ever been to a party with a lot of guests,
you know what it's like to be surrounded by
noise on every side. It can be a bit daunting, so
many people laughing and talking on top of each
other, particularly in a small space. Even under
the best of circumstances, it's tough to have a
heart-to-heart conversation with a friend amid
the overlapping of other voices.

That's how it is in life too. You're trying so
hard to hear God's voice, but the sound of all
the other voices is getting in the way. Friends,
your boss, the TV, the internet, social media,
the kids, schoolteachers, even emails. . .it's
just hard to focus on one thing when so many
things are babbling. Whew!

Part of the reason you get so frustrated
during hard times is because of these voices.

If you want to watch God work a real miracle, pull away and spend quiet time with Him. He longs to speak to you, to share His plan for your current struggle, but you'll never hear Him if you're not tuned in. That can only happen if you quiet those other voices. And remember those worries and cares you're holding on to? They're easy to let go of when you enter quiet time with the Lord.

There. Doesn't that feel good?

Lord, I need to pull away from the noise!
May I release my worries and concerns
today, Father, as I put my trust in You.
It's Your voice I want to hear. Amen.

Ripped Off

*Cast your burden on the LORD, and
he will sustain you; he will never
permit the righteous to be moved.*
PSALM 55:22 ESV

It's hard not to get angry when you've been
ripped off, isn't it? Kendra understood this
better than anyone. She hired a contractor to
help with the remodel of her home. Multiple
thousands of dollars later, he repeatedly returned to her for more money, but the work
wasn't getting done, at least not at the rate of
speed she'd hoped.

Kendra was even angrier when she learned
the contractor hadn't been paying his workers what he'd promised them. No wonder they
didn't want to show up to do the work! They were
angry too, and she didn't blame them. What had
he done with all the money she'd given him?
Was he pocketing it, perhaps?

Maybe you've been ripped off too. You've
dished out money to have a car repaired only

to find out it wasn't fixed at all. Or maybe you paid for someone to build your website, but you are unhappy with their sloppy work.

There are a lot of shady people out there, and it's easy to get angry or upset when you know you've been cheated. But God is still your Waymaker even when you've been taken advantage of. He can make things right quicker than you can say, "What's the number for the Better Business Bureau?" Take a deep breath. Cool down. Then lean on Him as you put together a plan of action.

Lord, I'll admit, I get pretty worked up when I've been taken advantage of. I don't like the way that feels. Show me how to best exemplify You even when I'm figuring out my next move. Amen.

The Breaking Point

*And let us not grow weary of
doing good, for in due season
we will reap, if we do not give up.*
GALATIANS 6:9 ESV

After a particularly long and exhausting morning with the kids, Anita heard a noise coming from the laundry room. She walked that way and was horrified to find the hose had come loose from the back of the washing machine, spilling hot water all over the floor. Worse still, she couldn't get to the hose because of the hot water. By the time she did, the floor and walls were saturated.

Tears streamed as she tried to figure out who to call first—the plumber, the flooring guy, or her husband. How in the world could she tackle a problem this big? On top of her already-crazy morning, this was just too much.

How many times have you cried out, "God, please take this! God, it's going to break me!"? God sees how close you are to the breaking

point, and He's standing there with arms extended, waiting for you to hand the problem to Him. He's not going to pry it out of your tightly clenched fingers. You have to open your palms and actually release your grip. It won't be easy, because you're such a fixer. But God will see you through in a way that you could never manage for yourself.

He will make a way out of the overwhelming seasons. Turn your eyes to Him today no matter how exhausted or distraught you might feel.

Lord, I'll admit I get overwhelmed easily. The worries, fears, and sorrows of those moments cause me to freeze in place. But I can trust You in the middle of the chaos, my Waymaker. Amen.

The Woman with the Issue of Blood

*And a woman was there who had been
subject to bleeding for twelve years, but no
one could heal her. She came up behind
him and touched the edge of his cloak,
and immediately her bleeding stopped.*

LUKE 8:43–44 NIV

If you've struggled with ongoing health issues—
autoimmune disease, disabilities, chronic pain,
or others—you know that things can eventually
reach a hopeless point. Well-meaning friends
and loved ones can say things like "Just keep
praying. It'll get better!" but you don't believe
them. Yet, there's this small part of you that
wants to.

Such was the case with the woman in the
Bible story found in the eighth chapter of Luke.
This poor woman had suffered with "an issue of
blood" (female hemorrhaging) for twelve long
years. Imagine. Twelve years of being ostracized

by others because of her painful condition.

When she heard that the Messiah was coming through, she had to get to Him. If she could just touch the hem of His garment, she would be healed. So, she pressed her way through the crowd until she grabbed the edge of His cloak. Immediately, Jesus froze in place and asked, "Who touched me?" He felt healing virtue go out of Him as she grabbed hold of His hem.

No matter how long you've waited, no matter how many times you've faced disappointment, your Waymaker will make a way through for you. Be like that tenacious woman. Don't give up. Push those worries aside, and press through the crowd until you reach Him. Then stretch out that arm to grab hold of all that He has for you.

Lord, I'm weary with battling health woes. Sometimes I feel like this is the way it's going to be. . .forever. No matter what I face, I know You're still my Waymaker. Help me to press my worries aside and lean in to You, Jesus. Amen.

A Ride You Never Meant to Take

This is what the LORD says—he who made a way through the sea, a path through the mighty waters, who drew out the chariots and horses, the army and reinforcements together, and they lay there, never to rise again, extinguished, snuffed out like a wick: "Forget the former things; do not dwell on the past. See, I am doing a new thing!"
ISAIAH 43:16–19 NIV

Casey had a recurring nightmare that involved a roller coaster, one she hadn't intended to board. She felt butterflies in her stomach as the car *click-click-clicked* its way to the top of the first hill. Then, with a *whoosh* that sent her stomach into her throat, it took off downhill. She let out a scream and held on for dear life as the coaster took her up and down, round and round, in all sorts of places she hadn't meant to go.

Maybe your life is like that roller coaster. At some point, you found yourself trapped in

a never-ending ride that has taken you places you never meant to go. You're at the mercy of the ones controlling the ride—your boss, your spouse, your friends—and you just want to get off, to do something different.

Even now, in the middle of that fear and worry, God is making a way out. This ride won't go on forever. He is your Waymaker when you feel trapped in a situation you didn't choose. He has new things planned for you. When you are released from the roller coaster, don't go backward! Keep moving forward into all He has for you.

*Lord, I won't worry about feeling trapped.
I know You can push the EJECT button anytime
You like. I'll trust You to do that and to make
a way into whatever You have next. Amen.*

Never-Ending Woes

*"I have said these things to you, that in me
you may have peace. In the world you
will have tribulation. But take heart;
I have overcome the world."*
JOHN 16:33 ESV

It's a wonderful feeling, having a freshly mowed lawn. It smells good, looks good, and you don't have to worry about any pesky letters from the homeowners' association chewing you out for letting things go. There's only one problem with a freshly cut lawn—it doesn't stay like that. In fact, the grass is growing even as you cut it.

Sometimes problems are like that too. You get a handle on them, you trim them back, and you breathe a sigh of relief, only to discover there are more problems springing up faster than you can keep up. Bills. Broken friendships. Job issues. Health problems. Marital woes. Problems with the kids. They're tiny blades of grass, creeping up around you, threatening to crowd out your joy and peace. Hard as you

136

try, you just can't keep up with their rapid-fire growth.

It's easy to get overwhelmed with the never-ending influx of issues that compound in your life. But think of God as a Master Gardener. He's plowing through those problems, cutting straight to the root, plucking them up as you are fretting over them. He's making a way through the very middle of them.

You can't handle the influx on your own. You were never meant to. Don't get overwhelmed.

Just trust Him. He will make a way.

Lord, sometimes life is just plain overwhelming. I solve one problem only to be faced with another. I deal with one issue, and two more pop up. I need Your help, Father. Make a way when I simply can't figure out my own way. Amen.

Political Feuds

Refrain from anger, and forsake wrath!
Fret not yourself; it tends only to evil.
PSALM 37:8 ESV

You were such good friends. . .before social media. Now you're getting irritated at all her political posts, and you're having a difficult time containing your frustration. It's not just the fact that she has an opposite viewpoint from yours; it's the frantic tone in her political posts and the way she snaps at folks who disagree with her. You didn't realize she was capable of such sarcasm or cruelty. And when did she become such a know-it-all?

On more than one occasion, you've wanted to call her on the carpet, to explain that she's doing more harm than good, that she's not doing a good job of representing Christ with her word choices or tone. But you know such a conversation would erupt into something much bigger.

It's not easy to maintain an amicable relationship with volatile people, especially when

you toss politics into the mix. And the enemy knows just how to fuel that fire, to separate friends and loved ones over political views.

Don't let him destroy your relationships. Unless the Lord specifically asks you to step away from a friend with a different political view, do all you can to live in peace. God has a way through these tough times, and it can all be summed up in one word: love. (Isn't it wonderful that your Waymaker uses love as a driving force?)

Show love to those with different opinions. Show love to those who seem to be seething with anger. Don't knee-jerk. Don't comment. Just keep scrolling. Pray. . .and love.

Father, You are my Waymaker during troublesome political times. I can trust You to make a way back to those I love, even the ones with vastly different views. Amen.

A Long March

*"Have I not commanded you? Be strong
and courageous. Do not be frightened,
and do not be dismayed, for the LORD
your God is with you wherever you go."*

JOSHUA 1:9 ESV

Why do you suppose God gave Joshua the command to march around the city of Jericho for seven days before He brought down the walls? The Lord could've done it in an instant, after all. But He chose to test Joshua's obedience, to see if this mighty man of God could make it through the final test before witnessing a miracle.

Isn't that just like the Lord, to involve His kids in the action? There you are, facing your Jericho. . .your enemy taunting you with a situation that threatens to destroy you. Instead of just knocking the walls down, which God could do with a word, He gives you a role to play. He tests your obedience by asking you to participate.

Maybe you don't want to participate. Perhaps you're hoping the Lord will just sweep in

and handle things for you. Your worry has you wound up so tightly you're not sure you can function. Do it anyway. (Or, as some would say, "Do it scared.")

Play the role you need to play. Do the thing you need to do. Then, when God does bring down those walls, you'll be able to look back on the situation and say, "I grew a lot through that trial."

Yes, He's your Waymaker. Yep, He'll see you through. But He wants your active participation so that you can grow in your faith every step of the way.

Okay, Lord! I'll do it. I'll march around my Jericho as many times as it takes to witness the miracle that You, my Waymaker, are preparing. Amen.

Natural Disasters

*Even though I walk through the valley
of the shadow of death, I will fear no
evil, for you are with me; your rod
and your staff, they comfort me.*

PSALM 23:4 ESV

Connie hunkered down in her closet with her husband and kids at her side. Outside, the storm raged. A category 4 hurricane threatened to steal everything they'd worked for. It shook the house, and the wind shrieked its way through the trees in the backyard. She pushed back tears and did her best to comfort her kids as the storm intensified directly overhead.

They heard a loud crack and then a crash.

"Mommy, what was that?"

"I don't know, baby." She glanced at her husband, who shook his head. No doubt a tree had come down. Connie prayed it hadn't done too much damage.

Maybe you've been there. You've hunkered down as a storm passed overhead. In those

hours, everything was out of your control. You couldn't see the damage until after the fact.

Life gives us all kinds of storms, and we have plenty of opportunity to worry and fret. They hit hard and fast and tear things apart that we've spent years building. They never play fair as they wreak havoc and cause destruction.

But God. . .

Don't you love those two words? God, your Waymaker, can quiet the storms. He can bring them to an end and make a way out of the destruction. Still your heart. Let the storm pass. Then trust Him to bring restoration and joy once again.

Lord, it's not always easy to trust in the storms, but You will make a way out for me when I fear all is lost. With You, all is never lost. I trust You, my Waymaker. Amen.

Responding in Obedience

Then God said, "Take your son, your only son, whom you love—Isaac—and go to the region of Moriah. Sacrifice him there as a burnt offering on a mountain I will show you."

GENESIS 22:2 NIV

What a conundrum Abraham faced! God had promised him a son. Years after the promise, Isaac arrived. He was the fulfillment of all the Lord said He would do. Why, then, would God ask Abraham to take that precious boy and sacrifice him as a burnt offering? It made no sense.

Abraham passed the test. He took faith steps and did all that the Lord asked of him, even at the risk of losing everything. In the end, God made a way out for Isaac. His life was spared because his father acted in obedience. Isaac went on to live an amazing life. He did great things for the Lord.

It's not easy to respond in obedience when you're faced with life-and-death situations. There are times when the things God asks you

to do make no sense at all, and you freeze in place, unable to comprehend His logic. But you can trust Him even in these confusing times. He will never ask you to do something that will bring you harm.

What are you going through right now? Is it causing you to worry and fret? Trust the Lord to make a way out, no matter how difficult. And remember, the choices you make today to trust the Lord will have an impact for generations to come.

I don't always get it, Lord. You tell me to do something, and at the time it makes no sense. But I'm learning! You always make a way out and teach me some amazing lessons along the way. I trust You, Father. Amen.

Global Upsets

Cast your burden on the LORD, and he will sustain you; he will never permit the righteous to be moved.
PSALM 55:22 ESV

The world has faced some major upsets in recent years—everything from weather-related catastrophes to a pandemic that has thrown everyone for a loop. There have been times when mankind has been frozen in place, petrified by all the chaos. It's hard to function when everyone around you is locked up with fear. The words *hunker down* are the only ones that come to mind. So, that's what you do. You turn your focus inward and curl up in a ball, hoping the storm passes quickly. Sometimes it does. . .and sometimes it doesn't.

Here's a biblical truth: You can still stand even when everyone around you is curled up in a ball, weeping. You can still proclaim your faith even when others are spouting fear or recoiling in anxiety. You can still lift high the banner

of peace even when others are spewing hate speech. In other words, you can be a reflection of Jesus in the midst of the global pandemic or any other crisis.

Don't be afraid. Don't worry. Yes, things are hard right now, but your Waymaker is longing to show you how to witness to others during the chaos that swirls around you. Someone needs to be a light. Someone needs to represent Him. Could that someone be you?

Lord, it feels like the world's gone crazy sometimes! I look around and don't recognize my own country anymore. But You, Lord, never change. In the midst of global unrest, You're right there, seated on Your throne and longing to use me, still. I am Your ready student, my Waymaker. Amen.

God's Multiplication

And he directed the people to sit down on the grass. Taking the five loaves and the two fish and looking up to heaven, he gave thanks and broke the loaves. Then he gave them to the disciples, and the disciples gave them to the people. They all ate and were satisfied, and the disciples picked up twelve basketfuls of broken pieces that were left over.

MATTHEW 14:19–20 NIV

Five loaves and two fishes. That's all he had in his little lunch sack. But the boy was willing to share when asked. He looked around, mesmerized by the crowd. There were thousands in attendance to hear this man Jesus speak. How could five loaves of bread and two little fishes feed so many?

The boy watched in awe as Jesus prayed over the food. . .and it multiplied! No matter how much food the disciples passed out, there was always plenty more. Was this some sort of magic trick? Some sort of multiplication miracle? The

boy couldn't understand it. Yet, his young heart was deeply touched by this man—the Messiah—who cared so much for the people.

God provided on that amazing day, and He's still in the "providing" business. You don't need to worry and fret when you're facing a crisis like the one the disciples faced that day. Your Waymaker already has an answer. He's going to impress the masses with what He does, wait and see! And you'll be right there, watching and trusting, just like that boy with the sack lunch.

In what area of your life would you like to see multiplication today? Trust the Lord to wow you as you place your hope in Him.

You're the great Multiplier, Lord! I love to watch You work. You can take something small and insignificant and turn it into something miraculous. Because I know You love to wow the people with Your multiplication skills, I know I can trust You to make a way, Father. Amen.

It Is Well with My Soul

You keep him in perfect peace whose mind is stayed on you, because he trusts in you.
ISAIAH 26:3 ESV

Horatio G. Spafford, author of the great hymn "It Is Well with My Soul," is perhaps one of our greatest historical examples of trusting God through seasons of pain. Horatio suffered many tragedies over the course of his life. His only son died. Then, in 1871, the great Chicago fire wiped out the family's real estate investments.

Horatio made the decision to take his family on a trip to Europe. Afterward, he was detained in Europe, but he sent his wife and four daughters on ahead. They boarded the SS *Ville du Havre* to sail home. Sadly, the ship went down at sea, killing many on board. His wife was miraculously saved, but all four of his beautiful daughters drowned.

Sometime later, Horatio traveled to the very spot where the ship went down and heard the Lord speaking consolation to his soul. He then

penned the words of the song "It Is Well with My Soul."

Somehow, in the midst of his pain, in the very middle of his anguish, the great Waymaker led him forward. God surely worked a miracle in the man's heart for him to be able to write the words: "Whatever my lot, thou hast taught me to say 'It is well, it is well with my soul.'"

Is it well with your soul today? If not, ask your precious Waymaker to lead you beyond the pain to a place of healing and restoration.

Lord, if Spafford could sing those words, if he could recover from so great a loss, I know I can get through the things that trouble me. May I say, "It is well with my soul!" no matter what I'm walking through, Father. Amen.

There Goes the Neighborhood

"Amid disquieting dreams in the night, when deep sleep falls on people, fear and trembling seized me and made all my bones shake."

JOB 4:13–14 NIV

When Debbie married her husband, Don, they were both deliriously happy and very much in love. They moved into their brand-new home a short time later. The neighborhood was just blossoming, and Debbie enjoyed getting to know the neighbors. There, in that precious place, she and Don raised their two children and remained as empty nesters when the kids moved on.

After Don passed away, Debbie was left with the feeling that the neighborhood, which had once been lovely and safe, was becoming something altogether different. The crime rate had increased, and she was starting to get nervous. Debbie couldn't bear the idea of leaving the house, but what could she do?

After several break-ins in nearby homes,

Debbie made the tough decision to move. Imagine her surprise when she found a darling little duplex that was perfect for her retirement years. She settled in quickly and celebrated the fact that everything felt new and unique to her.

God knows what you need and when you need it. He cares about every detail of your life, including your safety. So, trust Him when there are big decisions to be made about such things. He will help you make a way through the decisions and the fear. Let's face it—some of our fears are unfounded and don't require a big move, just the decision to let go of the fear.

No matter where you end up, trust your Waymaker to give you the very best.

Lord, I get scared sometimes. But I know You are my Protector, my Shield. I can trust You to squelch my fears and lead me to a place of safety, if necessary. I'm grateful for Your care. Amen.

I Just Can't Finish

*And I am sure of this, that he who
began a good work in you will bring it
to completion at the day of Jesus Christ.*
PHILIPPIANS 1:6 ESV

There are times in life when you simply don't
feel like you can finish what you've started.
Maybe you set out on an adventure to renovate
your home. About halfway in, you realize you're
in over your head. Just then the money runs out.
So you stop. You freeze in place because you're
overwhelmed and don't know what to do.

Or maybe you take on a challenge at work
then realize you don't really know enough to
carry it through. You're stuck and can't move
forward. It's embarrassing. . .and you wonder
if your boss will think you're incompetent. But
what can you do?

The enemy would love nothing more than
to stop you in your tracks, to convince you that
you aren't able to get the job done. But God
says otherwise! He doesn't just want you to be

a good starter; He wants you to be a woman who finishes well.

What areas of your life require finishing today? What have you started and left unattended? (Maybe too many things to count!) Today, make up your mind to tackle the very things you've been avoiding. God will make a way through any worries or concerns you might have as you plow forward. And guess what? He'll help you finish well!

Lord, I want to be known as a woman who finishes well. I don't want to start projects and not complete them. I'll need Your help with this one, Father. The enemy has done a stellar job of convincing me I don't have the goods. But You say otherwise, so I will listen to You, my Waymaker. Amen.

The Waiting List

Anxiety weighs down the heart,
but a kind word cheers it up.
PROVERBS 12:25 NIV

Maggie waited an extraordinary amount of time for her knee replacement surgery. It seemed the hospital could never get her on the schedule. Instead, they put her on the waiting list. So, she waited. And waited. And waited some more.

When the hospital personnel finally settled on a date, Maggie felt relieved. As the day grew near, though, she began to worry and fret. What would her life be like, she wondered, after the surgery? Would she heal in record time or struggle to walk for months on end like her friend Jean? Would she, like some, never be the same again?

So many fears and concerns gripped her as she thought it through. Primarily, she worried about the stairs in her home. How would she manage them as she headed up to her bedroom every night? And then there was the issue of

bathing herself. What if she slipped and fell? Who would come to her rescue?

Maybe you've been there too. You faced a medical hurdle and didn't think you could get past it. You wondered if your life would change for the better or worse.

Take heart! Even in the most difficult times, when you are bound with worries and fears, God is right there, ready to make a way for you. He wants you to know that He's still in the healing business and that He genuinely cares for you, His child. You can trust Him even now.

Lord, I've faced some pretty big obstacles over the years, but You've always proven yourself loving and faithful. May I not waver as hurdles come. Instead, I'll put my trust in You, my Waymaker. Amen.

Twelve Words

"In your anger do not sin": Do not let the
sun go down while you are still angry.
EPHESIANS 4:26 NIV

Amber was angry. Very angry. Her mother's
political post on social media was over the top
and just plain dumb. Amber had to educate
Mom immediately to prevent her from further
humiliating herself. Instead of reaching out
to her mom privately, she decided to give her
mother a piece of her mind publicly, right there
for everyone to see. And because her mom's
post was public, lots of people saw.

Before long, folks were chiming in from
every angle, some quite upset to see a young
woman publicly lashing out at her elderly
mother. Yikes. Amber suddenly felt ill that
she'd let her anger lead to divisive words. Sure,
proving her point on social media felt good
in the moment, but what if this was the last
conversation she ever had with her mother?

Would she feel content, knowing their final words had been spoken in anger?

Maybe you've been there. You've entered a divisive conversation only to regret it later. Now there are walls between you and your loved one. You're wishing things were different. But how can you mend fences?

God is a Waymaker and can mend even the toughest situation. He does ask a couple things of you: to walk humbly and to repent if you've wronged someone (even going to that person to make things better). The best twelve words you can speak to a loved one you've wronged are these: "I am sorry. I was wrong. I love you. Please forgive me." You'll be stunned at how quickly God can use those twelve words to bring healing.

Father, I'll admit I've let my temper get the best of me. I've let walls of separation grow up between myself and my loved ones. Now I'd love for those walls to come down. Please make a way, Lord. Please let this division end. Amen.

A Godly Resolution

And above all these put on love, which binds everything together in perfect harmony. And let the peace of Christ rule in your hearts, to which indeed you were called in one body. And be thankful.
COLOSSIANS 3:14–15 ESV

After years of hiding Jewish people in their family home, Corrie ten Boom and her family members were arrested and sent to a concentration camp. While there, she witnessed untold atrocities. Her precious sister grew ill and died, making the situation even more unbearable.

Somehow, Corrie found a way to get through it all, keeping her focus on God and on others around her. She refused to give in to depression or anger, and she kept her gaze on her Waymaker, who eventually led her to complete freedom. Once released, she became known world-round as she shared her Christ-centered testimony.

It's so hard to witness cruelty and injustice

happening in this world around us. We want to lash out, to say all sorts of things, to stir things up. But sometimes it's the quiet, simple faith of someone like Corrie that makes the most difference. Godly resolutions can come if we just keep our cool and ask for the mind of Christ. It's not easy, especially if you factor in your emotions, but it is possible.

Are you witnessing injustices? Do they make you angry? Pause and ask God how you can make a difference. And remember, He'll never ask you to do something that will hurt someone else. So, take a deep breath before you dive in. Above all, put on love. It's the great diffuser and will make a lasting difference.

Lord, I want to make a difference,
to end injustice in the world. But I don't
want to hurt others in my attempt. Please
show me Your way, Father. Make a way
for me to act. . .but not react. Amen.

Resurrection Power

After Jesus said this, he cried out in a loud voice,
"Lazarus, come out!" The dead man came out,
his hands and feet wrapped with pieces of cloth,
and a cloth around his face.

JOHN 11:43–44 NCV

It's one thing to have a near-death experience.
It's another thing altogether to actually die. . .
and then come back to life.

It's impossible to imagine what Lazarus
must've been thinking as Jesus called him forth
out of the tomb. Was he already enjoying the
beauties of heaven? Had the experience been
otherworldly? If so, he might've preferred to
stay put! But God had other plans for Lazarus.
He used him as a vivid demonstration of His
resurrection power.

The Lord is still in the business of bringing
people back from the brink. What if something
dark and horrible you're walking through right
now—in this very moment—could be used to
show others the light and life of Christ? Would

it all be worth it? What if God wanted to bring you back from the brink of something tragic to prove His resurrection power? Would you be willing to make the journey with Him?

No matter where you are today, anticipate God's resurrection power. He can, with the blink of an eye, change your situation and use it for good, not just in your life but in the lives of those who are watching. Your Waymaker is going to use your story, your testimony, your life to reach others with the Gospel message. No matter where you are today, begin to anticipate His resurrection power. He will provide a way out and an amazing testimony as well.

Lord, I'm longing for You to resurrect me from this situation I'm going through. Bring life from death. Bring beauty from ashes. Bring hope from hopelessness. Amen.

The Lions' Den

Daniel decided not to eat the king's food or drink his wine because that would make him unclean. So he asked Ashpenaz for permission not to make himself unclean in this way.
DANIEL 1:8 NCV

We think we have it pretty bad these days. Our religious freedoms seem to be slipping away. Our ability to share the biblical message is often censored by social media police. It's getting harder and harder to take a stand for our faith.

But then again, we'll never have it as rough as Daniel! He was thrown into a lions' den for breaking the law. What law? He continued to pray to the one true God even after being forbidden to do so. He refused to give up his faith, so into the lions' den he went, where he found himself face-to-face with hungry beasts!

God spared Daniel's life. He kept the lions' jaws shut, and Daniel survived the ordeal. You'll survive too. If the great Waymaker intervened in Daniel's situation, He will intervene in yours.

Count on it. Does this mean you won't encounter persecution? No. In this day and age, you will most likely experience it, but you'll come through it without any teeth marks in your flesh.

Don't let anyone keep you from speaking truth. Don't let anyone keep you from believing the Bible. Don't allow anyone to keep you from praying. God will honor your faith if you'll just keep standing. With your Waymaker's power, you can do just that.

Lord, I won't worry about what's going to happen to me. I'll keep speaking the truth in love and count on You to protect me. If You did it for Daniel, You'll do it for me. Amen.

Erratic Behaviors

The LORD is a stronghold for the oppressed,
a stronghold in times of trouble.
PSALM 9:9 ESV

Leigh struggled to get along with her mother much of her life. Mom's behavior was erratic and a little off-the-wall at times. It wasn't until Leigh was grown that she realized her mother was dealing with mental illness. It was affecting every area of her life—her job, relationships, and even her finances.

Once this was discovered, Leigh was able to calm down and see the situation differently. In other words, her reactions to her mother's erratic behavior changed, which helped diffuse the situations that cropped up. She tried to see her mother's struggles through God's eyes, which kept her from overreacting when Mom did something irrational.

Maybe you're dealing with someone whose behavior is perplexing at best. She startles people with her behaviors, and you're at a loss to

know how to respond. You tend to react, which only makes things worse. Today, try to see that person and their struggles through God's eyes. Ask for His vision, His clarity. Then pray that your loved one will be healed mentally, physically, and emotionally.

Isn't that what you really want? It's not enough to win an argument with a loved one or to prove a point. What you really want is true and lasting healing, and that begins with love and understanding. Only your Waymaker can give you that. So, lay down those worries, and trust Him to make a way through this tricky situation.

Lord, I'll stop worrying about those I cannot fix. Their problems and issues are in Your hands. You're the only One who can heal heart, mind, body, and spirit. Move in my loved one's life today, I pray. Amen.

Lost Sheep

So he told them this parable: "What man of you, having a hundred sheep, if he has lost one of them, does not leave the ninety-nine in the open country, and go after the one that is lost, until he finds it? And when he has found it, he lays it on his shoulders, rejoicing."
LUKE 15:3–5 ESV

Nancy paced the front hallway of her home, completely distraught. News of her daughter's arrest was almost more than she could take. Presley had a drug problem. She'd been struggling with it for years. But to reach this point. . .where she'd actually been arrested for being under the influence while driving? How terrifying. Nancy's only solace was the fact that no one had been injured as a result of her daughter's behaviors. No one other than her daughter, that is.

Maybe you know what it's like to watch a beloved child take a tumble. It's heartbreaking. You can't picture your precious, innocent little

daughter shifting so far from the way she was raised. You didn't teach her to take drugs or consume too much alcohol. You certainly didn't raise her to have a temper or to abuse her child. How did this happen?

It's hard not to worry when your child is walking down the wrong path. You imagine all sorts of scenarios in your mind about how her story will end. But God wants you to know that He's already planned a way out for your loved one. There's a role for your child to play, of course, but fretting and nagging won't nudge her in the right direction. Taking your hands off will be one of the hardest things you've ever had to do, but the Lord will make a way once you do.

Lord, I want to fix everything, but there are some things that I can't touch. I must leave them in Your hands. For all of my loved ones in trouble, I beg for Your intervention. Help them find a way back to You, I pray. Amen.

Budget Shifts

"Take my yoke upon you, and learn from me, for I am gentle and lowly in heart, and you will find rest for your souls. For my yoke is easy, and my burden is light."
MATTHEW 11:29–30 ESV

Lorena waited anxiously in the car salesman's office while he went to talk to the manager. She twisted her hands together, anxious at all she was facing and unsure about the decisions at hand. To take on a new car payment right now wasn't in her plans, but when the transmission went out on her old vehicle, she had no choice. Hours of prayer had gone into this decision. . .and now she waited.

The salesman returned to the office a short time later, all smiles. "Well, I think I have some news that's going to make you very happy." He went on to give her the terms of her loan. She breathed a sigh of relief when she saw that the payments on the new vehicle weren't going to be as high as expected.

She could manage this with God's help.

Maybe you've had to take on a new payment like Lorena. It took some juggling to figure out if your budget could handle the strain, but in the end, you had no other choice.

Even when it comes to the big things—mortgages, rent, car payments, insurance, and so on—God sees and cares. If He cares about the sparrows and the creepy-crawly critters, how much more does He care about you? He will provide for all you need.

Lord, I don't like financial woes. They trouble my soul. But I can trust You with financial decisions, even the big ones. You're making a way to cover all my needs, and I'm so grateful. Amen.

Led by the Spirit

And Jesus, full of the Holy Spirit, returned from the Jordan and was led by the Spirit in the wilderness for forty days, being tempted by the devil. And he ate nothing during those days. And when they were ended, he was hungry.

LUKE 4:1–2 ESV

Can you even begin to imagine all that Jesus went through as He stayed in the desert for forty days with no food or water to sustain Him? There, in the very middle of His physical weakness, the devil came to Him to tempt Him. That slippery devil did all he could to torment our Savior and bend His will, but Jesus wouldn't budge.

Isn't that just like the enemy? He waits until you're worn down and then comes at you, tormenting, pressuring, accusing. You're so depleted, you don't know how to respond.

Take a closer look at Luke 4:1. Notice a key phrase? "Jesus. . .was led by the Spirit." The Spirit of God longs to lead you too, especially

when you feel you can't go on. With a gentle nudge, He can move you in the direction you need to go. Yes, the voice of the enemy will still ring out, but you don't need to worry about that. You have an internal GPS guiding and leading you. Your Waymaker is at work even when you can't think straight. Even when you're wiped out. Even when you're being tormented mentally and physically.

Can you hear His voice? Lean in close. Block out the shouts going on around you. There it is! The Lord is speaking.

Lord, I'm so grateful for Your still, small voice, especially when the enemy is after me, trying to wear me down. I will trust You to guide me. You're my Waymaker even in the desert, Lord. Amen.

The Medical Journey

*And Jesus answered them, "Those who
are well have no need of a physician,
but those who are sick."*

LUKE 5:31 ESV

So many things about her medical journey drove
Pam crazy. First, she struggled to find health
insurance. Being self-employed, she had to
take out a private policy, which was far more
expensive than she'd bargained for. She swal-
lowed hard as she chose a policy that was nearly
as high as her monthly mortgage. Then, she had
trouble finding a doctor who would take her
insurance. Would this nightmare never end?

Once she finally settled on a doctor, he re-
tired and left the practice. It took some work,
but she found another just about the time she
came down with the flu. Little did she realize
how much that flu would cost her. Between
the deductibles, copays, and prescriptions—not
to mention the time lost from work—she was

up to her eyeballs in medical bills.

Maybe you've fretted over medical issues too. You've struggled to find coverage or to locate a doctor. You've been faced with unexpected bills and don't know how they'll get paid.

Even in the midst of major medical woes, God is still there. He hasn't fallen off His throne. He's making a way, carving a path in the wilderness. The Lord cares about you and won't leave you without the help you need. Trust Him. Pray for direction. Then watch as your Waymaker guides you to the care and coverage you need.

Lord, this is a big one. I've had to make some hard decisions in my life, but finding the right medical care hasn't been easy. I trust You to lead me to the very places I need to go. Amen.

Walking on Water

*And in the fourth watch of the night he came to
them, walking on the sea. But when the disciples
saw him walking on the sea, they were terrified,
and said, "It is a ghost!" and they cried out
in fear. But immediately Jesus spoke to them,
saying, "Take heart; it is I. Do not be afraid."*
MATTHEW 14:25–27 ESV

Janie loved to swim and was so grateful to grow
up with a pool in the backyard. She learned to
do all sorts of tricks in the water—everything
from handstands to flips to acrobatics off the
diving board. One thing she never conquered,
however, was walking on water. She would step
off the side of the pool, fully expecting her feet
to grace the top of the water only, but down she
would go—*glub, glub, glub*. Still, she never gave
up trying. Perhaps one day she would manage it.

If you actually saw someone walking on
the water, no doubt you'd be flabbergasted.
Imagine how the disciples felt when they saw
Jesus walking toward them on the sea. They

thought He was a ghost! But the Savior used that opportunity to teach them a lesson—that even the impossible is possible with God.

Maybe you're in a sinking season. You feel like everything around you is going down, down, down to the bottom of the sea. You can't imagine the Lord could revive what's been lost. Don't forget, God is a Waymaker! He can make a way even when your dreams have sunk to the depths. With one breath, He'll have you up, walking on water, ready to take on the world. Like Janie, you won't manage it on your own. But with God's hand in yours, you truly can walk on water.

I'm going to try it, Lord! I'm going to increase my faith and step out toward You even when it feels like I might sink. I'm trusting You to make a way across the waters. Amen.

Neighborly Disputes

There is no fear in love, but perfect love casts out fear. For fear has to do with punishment, and whoever fears has not been perfected in love.
1 John 4:18 esv

Athena's neighbor left a note on the door, complaining about the dog. Again. She couldn't seem to get the pooch to stop digging holes under the fence, and it was grating on her neighbor's nerves. Not that she blamed him. It frustrated her too. She did everything in her power to fill the holes and repair any damage, and then she baked some homemade peanut butter cookies for her neighbor. It turned out he was allergic.

There's nothing worse than a dispute with neighbors. If things don't get settled, tough feelings can lead to divisions that last for months, even years. And worse still, folks around you—other neighbors—might begin to take sides, to put up proverbial walls. Talk about awkward!

God never intended for folks to live in a

divided state. His desire has always been unity and love. The Bible is filled with scriptures to drive home that point. And yet. . .living in harmony seems to be nearly impossible at times.

Take a look at those around you. Think of the neighbor who's the hardest to live with. What can you do to tear down any walls or to bring true and lasting peace? The Lord always has a way out of relational issues, even the ones that have you bound up with worry. He will make a way through the dispute if you ask Him to.

I don't like division, Lord! Once those walls go up, it feels like the relationship is truly over. I can't imagine how I can fix the situation. But You, my Waymaker, can tear down walls! You can soften hearts and heal pain. Show me how to move in mercy and forgiveness so that walls will come down, I pray. Amen.

Resurrection of a Dream

Jesus said to her, "I am the resurrection and the life. Whoever believes in me, though he die, yet shall he live, and everyone who lives and believes in me shall never die. Do you believe this?"
JOHN 11:25–26 ESV

Have you ever thought about the resurrection of Jesus from His point of view? What was going on in that tomb after His death? Whatever Jesus experienced between His crucifixion and resurrection, He committed to come back—to prove His story to all His followers.

And come back, He did! The stone was rolled away, and the tomb was empty. Jesus was no longer there. Still, you might wonder what He was thinking and feeling as He rose from the dead. It would be fascinating to understand all He went through from the moment of death until the moment of resurrection.

Maybe you've been through seasons where you felt entombed. You felt dead inside. Your dreams died. Your relationships dwindled. Your

job situation fell apart. Instead of life, you experienced deep-seated grief.

Then, in one fell swoop, God rolled away the stone and brought you back to life again. He supplied your needs in a remarkable way. In place of the old job, a newer, better one. In place of an empty pantry, one stocked and ready.

God is a Waymaker even when you're in the tomb. He's just as ready, just as willing, just as able when you're at the bottom of the well as when you're on the mountaintop. Don't give up. Think of what happened to Jesus in the tomb. There's new life coming, and it's going to make the old one pale in comparison.

Lord, I do feel entombed at times. I wonder if You'll ever breathe life into these bones once again. Will You rebirth my dreams, my opportunities, my friendships? Will You roll away the stone and offer a complete rebirth? That's what I long for, Father. Amen.

Missing Out

You keep him in perfect peace whose mind is
stayed on you, because he trusts in you.
ISAIAH 26:3 ESV

From the time she was a little girl, Lisa knew exactly what she wanted to be when she grew up—a marine biologist. Ask her any question about her future, and she knew the answer. But when she turned eighteen, something catastrophic happened. Her parents were killed in a car accident, and she was left to raise her two younger siblings on her own.

Her dream of going to college was delayed by several years. Once she finally had the opportunity, the local junior college was the best she could manage financially. She juggled her classes, taking many at night to accommodate her siblings' busy schedules.

Nothing in Lisa's life turned out exactly as she had planned, and she fretted over the losses on a regular basis. Only when her siblings were grown and married did she realize the

truth—God had given her a far greater education than she could have ever received on her own. Along the way, she developed a passion for caring for others. So, when she finally transferred to the university, she chose a completely different major—that of psychologist.

Isn't it remarkable to know that God has big plans for us, sometimes bigger than we can see for ourselves? If you're feeling the pain of a lost dream today, ask your Waymaker to give you eyes to see an even bigger dream. Chances are He's up to something far beyond anything you might have imagined.

Father, I have dreams, sure. But they don't come close to what You have in mind for me. I won't mourn my losses for long, Lord. Instead, I'll look ahead to what You have planned. Amen.

A Contest on the Mountain

*"LORD, answer my prayer so these people
will know that you, LORD, are God and
that you will change their minds."*

1 KINGS 18:37 NCV

Elijah, a prophet of God, challenged the prophets of Baal (a false god) to see which was the one true God. He instructed them to build an altar and to lay a sacrificial bull on it. Then they were to call on their false god to light the altar on fire.

With much enthusiasm, the false prophets began the games! They begged Baal for hours, but nothing happened. You can imagine their disappointment. Then Elijah prepared an altar of wood. He placed a bull on it and instructed the men to douse the whole thing in water three times until it was fully saturated. Then he called out to the one true God, and the Lord responded by lighting the altar on fire and consuming it.

Surely, Elijah's knees were knocking (at least a little bit) when he called on God. He may have had moments of doubt. But his Waymaker

came through and proved, once and for all, that He was and is the only true and living God.

Maybe you've had to stand in faith in a situation that looked impossible. You did your best to trust and believe. And the Lord God—your Waymaker—proved Himself once again. He loves to do that, you know. You can trust Him even in impossible situations. And when the world doubts it, just step back and let the Lord prove it Himself.

Lord, You've done some pretty remarkable things! You made a way for Elijah that must've wowed the masses! You're still as powerful even now. Increase my faith as I face the doubters, Father. Amen.

Why Do the Wicked Prosper?

I tried to understand all this, but it was too hard for me to see until I went to the Temple of God. Then I understood what will happen to them.

PSALM 73:16–17 NCV

Have you ever felt like you're going through four seasons of winter? Everything around you has dried up, and you wonder if spring will ever arrive. As you wipe the frost from your windows and peer outside, you notice others going on with their lives surrounded by sunshine and joyful days. How can this be? It doesn't seem fair. Why are you trapped, frozen in place, as they celebrate joyous, carefree days?

Worse still, the ones celebrating are the evil ones! You've seen how they live. They haven't dedicated their lives to the Lord like you have. They have partied and been unfaithful—to spouses, friends, and family. And yet, somehow, they always seem to come out on top.

Take a good look at Psalm 73. Read the whole chapter from start to finish. David asks the same

questions you're asking: "Why do the wicked prosper?" (Hey, it's a legitimate question!)

At the midway point of the psalm, the tone shifts. David realizes that these ungodly people might have it good now, but their joys are temporary. They won't come to a happy end.

It's time to shift your focus. It's time to reach those who need to be reached with the Gospel message. Instead of fretting over how much better they have it now, shift your focus to what you'll one day have, then share the Good News so that they can have that too. God will make a way for you out of the worries and cares you're currently facing to the joys of heaven.

I want to be a light for those who don't know You, Father. Even the ones I'm jealous of. Especially the ones I'm jealous of. You'll make a way out of my worries once I begin to see them through Your eternal vision, Lord. Help me to do that, I pray. Amen.

Praise Your Way Through

Through him then let us continually
offer up a sacrifice of praise to God, that is,
the fruit of lips that acknowledge his name.
HEBREWS 13:15 ESV

You're exhausted. You've really been through it. You've been beaten down in life, and it has drained every ounce of strength from you. The last thing you feel like doing is lifting up a song of praise. Who has the time or energy for that?

Oh, but that's exactly when you should praise the Lord, when you don't feel like it! The finest way to press through your worries and watch God work is by praising Him. In doing so, you'll find a way out of the things that are depleting you.

Sure, it's not going to be easy to lift those hands in praise, not with the battle raging around you. You certainly won't feel like it. But isn't that what Moses was asked to do in the midst of the battle—to keep his arms lifted in praise? He called on godly friends to

help. Maybe you need to do that too. Ask your friends, your children, your Bible study group to stand with you in praise as you power your way through whatever traumas you're facing.

You'll get through this. God always makes a way. But it's much more fun to soar through with words of praise on your lips.

I don't feel like it, Lord. I'm so weary. But I will lift up a song and a shout of praise even now. You're making a way through my weariness as I shift my focus to You. That's exactly what I need, Father! Thank You. Amen.

God Hasn't Fallen off His Throne

When the cares of my heart are many,
your consolations cheer my soul.
PSALM 94:19 ESV

When you think about God—the Almighty Author of all—seated on His throne, what do you see? Is your perspective of Him the same in good times and bad?

Here's the truth: God doesn't fall off His throne when the rough days come. He's not struggling to keep His proverbial crown in place. The scepter hasn't slipped out of His hand. He's just as ready to rule in hard times as He is in easy ones. And as long as He's seated on the throne, you can trust that His role in your life and your struggles will be completed just as He sees fit.

God is still just as capable, just as willing; you can trust Him no matter what you're going through. Picture Him, even now, extending His

hand and saying, "Come, child! Sit at My feet and visit with Me awhile. Get My perspective. Experience My love. I won't let you down. I never have and I never will. Trust Me with your journey. I know the way. I can see clearly down the road ahead. I will make a way for you because I adore you!"

When you stick close to Him, you'll be reminded afresh of His great love for you. And every worry, every concern will drift away like the feathery wisps of a dandelion on the wind.

God, You are firmly seated on Your throne, never wavering! What peace this gives me! No matter what I face, no matter what troubles my mind, You're not anxious or upset. You already have the answers to my problems, and You're showing me the way. How grateful I am to You, my Waymaker! Amen.

About the Author

Janice Thompson, who lives in the Houston area, writes novels, nonfiction, magazine articles, and musical comedies for the stage. The mother of four married daughters, she is quickly adding grandchildren to the family mix.